Financing Americas Leadership

Protecting American
Interests and Promoting
American Values

OTHER COUNCIL ON FOREIGN RELATIONS
TASK FORCE REPORTS

Rethinking International Drug Control:
New Directions for U.S. Policy (1997)
   Mathea Falco, Chair

A New U.S. Policy Toward India and Pakistan (1997)
   Richard N. Haass, Chairman; Gideon Rose, Project Director

Arms Control and the U.S.-Russian Relationship:
Problems, Prospects, and Prescriptions (1996)
   Robert D. Blackwill, Chairman and Author
   Keith W. Dayton, Project Director

American National Interests and the United Nations (1996)
   George Soros, Chairman

Making Intelligence Smarter: The Future of U.S. Intelligence (1996)
   Maurice R. Greenberg, Chairman
   Richard N. Haass, Project Director

Lessons of the Mexican Peso Crisis (1996)
   John C. Whitehead, Chairman
   Marie-Josee Kravis, Project Director

Non-Lethal Technologies: Military Options and Implications (1995)
   Malcolm H. Wiener, Chairman

Managing the Taiwan Issue:
Key Is Better U.S. Relations with China (1995)
   Stephen Friedman, Chairman
   Elizabeth Economy, Project Director

Should NATO Expand? (1995)
   Harold Brown, Chairman; Charles Kupchan, Project Director

Success or Sellout? The U.S.-North Korean Nuclear Accord (1995)
   Kyung Won Kim and Nicholas Platt, Chairmen
   Richard N. Haass, Project Director

Nuclear Proliferation: Confronting the New Challenges (1995)
   Stephen J. Hadley, Chairman; Mitchell B. Reiss, Project Director

---

*Available from Brookings Institution Press ($5.00 per copy).
To order, call 1–800–275–1447.

Financing America's Leadership

Protecting American Interests and Promoting American Values

Report of an Independent Task Force

Sponsored by the Brookings Institution
and the Council on Foreign Relations

Mickey Edwards and Stephen J. Solarz,
Co-Chairmen

Morton H. Halperin, Lawrence J. Korb,
and Richard M. Moose, Project Directors

CONTENTS

ACKNOWLEDGMENTS

WE WISH to thank a number of individuals whose work contributed to the project. Susan Lynne Tillou at the Council on Foreign Relations, Washington, D.C., facilitated and maintained communication among the more than 150 Task Force members and other participants during the major life of the project, including the review and production stages. Kristen Lomasney, her predecessor at the project's inception, helped get the project started and provided advice throughout.

At the Brookings Institution, Michael O'Hanlon, assisted by Carol Graham, prepared the Background Study in an effort to explain and support the recommendations and thinking of the Task Force. Others who assisted in this work were Christina Larson and Susan Hardesty at the Brookings Institution and Sheila Roquitte at Princeton University.

Without the generous support of the John F. Kennedy School of Government in Cambridge and the Washington Council on International Trade (WCIT) in Seattle, the discussion meetings in those two cities would not have been possible. In particular, we appreciated the assistance of Patricia Davis, Barbara Hazzard, and Nancy Dye of the WCIT in organizing the Seattle meeting. David K.Y. Tang, a Council on Foreign Relations member in Seattle, chaired those discussions, and his firm, Preston, Gates & Ellis, generously hosted the breakfast meeting.

The Cambridge dinner meeting was arranged and underwritten by the John F. Kennedy School under the sponsorship of its dean, Joseph S. Nye, Jr., and with support from Mark Burns, Jessica Hobart, Celes Eckerman Hughes, Adam Grissom, Paula Jacobson, Sarah Lischer, and Jeremy Zucker, who also assisted Co-Chairman Edwards. In Washington, Bobbi Avancena facilitated Co-Chairman Solarz's participation and supported the Task Force in many ways.

We are also grateful to Michael Holtzman, who handled public relations for the Task Force from the Council on Foreign Relations office in New York, and Colin Wheeler of the Council's National Program, who assisted with the Cambridge and Seattle meetings.

Finally, we wish to express our particular thanks to the project directors. The Task Force is grateful for the invaluable insight and comprehensive knowledge provided by Lawrence J. Korb of the Brookings Institution and Morton H. Halperin and Richard M. Moose of the Council on Foreign Relations.

Mickey Edwards
The John F. Kennedy
School of Government

Stephen J. Solarz
APCO Associates

FOREWORD

THE INDEPENDENT Task Force on resources for international relations was chaired by former Representatives Mickey Edwards and Stephen J. Solarz. The initiative that led to the creation of the Task Force came from the Brookings Institution and the Council on Foreign Relations. Members of the Task Force were asked to assess the consequences of the declining trend in funding for the conduct of international relations and to make such recommendations as they saw fit. The membership of the Task Force included a number of former officials of previous administrations as well as other prominent Americans with a deep interest in international affairs.

The members of the Task Force met three times in Washington. Meetings with interested citizens were also held in Boston and Seattle. In the course of its deliberations, the Task Force consulted with officials of the executive branch, members of Congress, and other knowledgeable individuals. The Statement that follows sets forth the findings and recommendations of the Task Force, but a number of other individuals, including those who participated in the Boston and Seattle meetings, were offered the opportunity to sign the Statement—and many did. Only private citizens were asked to endorse the Statement.

We thank and commend them for their effort and Report and hope it will stimulate congressional and public debate on a matter of great importance to our nation.

Michael H. Armacost
President
The Brookings Institution

Leslie H. Gelb
President
Council on Foreign Relations

Statement of the Task Force

INTRODUCTION AND SUMMARY

RELATIVE TO THE AVERAGE of the 1980s, U.S. spending on international affairs has fallen nearly 20 percent in real terms, and it could decline by as much as another 30 percent under the plans proposed by the president and the 104th Congress for balancing the federal budget by 2002.

Noting this trend in foreign affairs spending, the Council on Foreign Relations and the Brookings Institution, while taking no positions on the question as organizations, convened an independent Task Force of distinguished private citizens with a strong commitment to foreign affairs to examine consequences of the trend and to make such recommendations as it might see fit.[1]

The Task Force concludes that the cuts already made in the international affairs discretionary account have adversely affected, to a significant degree, the ability of the United States to protect and promote its economic, diplomatic, and strategic agendas abroad. Unless this trend is reversed, American vital interests will be jeopardized.

The Task Force calls on the president and the secretary of state to exert the strong and sustained leadership that will be necessary to secure the understanding of the American people and the bipartisan support of Congress to provide the funds necessary to finance American global leadership. This effort must be accompanied by a thorough review of the foreign affairs agencies with an eye toward

---

[1] This Statement reflects the general policy thrust and judgments reached by the group, although not all members of the group necessarily subscribe to every finding and recommendation in this Statement.

a structure and processes that will be more efficient and effective in terms of today's requirements.[2]

The Task Force recommends that the president call for an increase in international affairs spending from its level of about $19 billion in 1997 to $21 billion in 1998, with annual adjustments through the year 2002 to offset projected inflation.[3] In addition, this Report calls for the creation of a bipartisan commission to consider possible reforms in the State Department and the other foreign affairs agencies and substantial achievable economies in existing programs and budgets. The amount of the net increase the Task Force proposes represents only about one-tenth of one percent of the entire fiscal year (FY) 1997 federal budget and less than four-tenths of one percent of the total discretionary budget. Although these amounts are small in absolute terms, the potential consequences of not having them are quite large.

THE CHALLENGE AND OPPORTUNITY

WITH THE COLD WAR over, it is natural that the United States should focus more on domestic concerns. Reducing the federal budget deficit must be a high priority. Ensuring that government programs are efficient and effective is an obligation owed to American taxpayers. However, domestic renewal must not blind us to the world's continuing dangers and the requirements of America's essential leadership role.

The end of the Cold War has transformed the nature of the challenges that face the United States. Ethnic strife, regional instability, crime, narcotics, terrorism, famine, environmental degradation, fanaticism, and rogue regimes with mass destruction capabilities have

---

[2] Since the Statement was completed, the president submitted his budget for fiscal year 1998. It would slow, but not stop, the ongoing decline in real spending for international affairs. (Please see selected budget text in the Background Materials section of this Report.)

[3] The corresponding amount of budget authority would be roughly $22 billion in 1998 due to the fact that increases in actual spending always lag behind increases in the authorization to spend. The amounts are similar to, but for technical reasons somewhat greater than, spending and budget authority for the "150 (foreign affairs) account."

taken the place of the global Communist threat on our agenda. The United States cannot effectively protect its interests in these areas and provide leadership for those who would work with us unless we are prepared to spend the amount necessary to protect our interests and promote our values.

Moreover, by strengthening friendly forces and by calming and defusing potentially explosive situations, our diplomats can reduce the demands upon our military forces, avoid unnecessary troop deployments, and save much more money in the defense account than would be spent from the much smaller foreign affairs account. With such objectives in mind, our diplomatic arm, for example, has reinforced in recent years our basic Asia-Pacific alliances with Japan, Korea, Australia, Thailand, and the Philippines. In both Asia and Europe, new concepts of regional security and economic cooperation have been advocated, including dialogues among former adversaries. Timely spending for conflict resolution can help to obviate the need for costly disaster relief, refugee resettlement, and possible military deployments.

The U.S. economy is increasingly interdependent with the rest of the world—a world that is increasingly competitive. Most recent increases in our nation's manufacturing employment have come from increased export volume that has produced jobs with higher than average wages and helped to drive the continuous growth of our economy. Our ability to sustain that growth depends, in part, on our willingness and ability to employ the traditional instruments of foreign policy to promote exports, protect our products, and ensure open trade. These are complex undertakings that include tasks ranging from sustainable development and basic institution building (e.g., establishing commercial codes where none have existed) to multilateral trade negotiations, such as in the World Trade Organization. We know how to do these things; we must establish the priorities and be prepared to spend the money to deploy the assets, people, and institutions required to achieve them.

Managing today's international, political, economic, and security problems and seizing the opportunities before us requires American leadership. Exercising that leadership is difficult. It demands sustained official and public diplomacy, an array of economic and military sticks and carrots, and preventive measures where they can be effective. And it will require money.

Senator Richard Lugar in a recent admonition to the country's policymakers summarized the view of the Task Force:

> Too many leaders in both political parties have bowed to political expedience and embraced the fiction that international spending does not benefit Americans and therefore can be cut with impunity. As important as balancing the budget is, it will not happen if American disengagement from the world results in nuclear terrorism, an international trade war, an international energy crisis, a major regional conflict requiring U.S. intervention, or some other preventable disaster that undermines our security and prosperity.

Americans want the United States to remain a world leader. Polling by the Chicago Council on Foreign Relations reveals that two-thirds of the public wants the United States to remain actively engaged in world affairs. The number is actually higher than during the 1970s and early 1980s, when the United States was in the winter of the Cold War. Other poll data strongly support the belief that the public is willing to pay for continued global engagement.

PROJECTED EXPENDITURES

WHAT RESOURCES is our government currently devoting to meeting these global challenges and opportunities?

In FY 1997, the United States will spend about $19 billion for its diplomatic and foreign assistance. That amount is slightly more than one percent of the overall federal budget. It is less in real or inflation-adjusted terms than international discretionary spending in any year since 1979 and nearly 20 percent below the average since then.

International affairs is the only major category of federal spending that has undergone a real reduction since 1980. Along with funding for the Pentagon, international spending is one of only two major components of the federal budget to have been reduced since 1990.

As problematic as spending cuts have been to date, those now planned are much worse. The president's fiscal plan of early 1996

[4]

anticipated that real funding for international affairs would decline from $19 billion to $16.5 billion by 2002.[4] If he agrees—as he may do—to use Congressional Budget Office assumptions, the president would need to cut significantly more. Under the congressional budget-balancing resolution of April 1996, international spending would have dropped to $13 billion, or 30 percent below its current level and 45 percent below its 1980–95 average in constant 1997 dollars. That would be less than at any time since 1955.

In contrast with the defense and intelligence budgets, the international affairs account is not at all protected in the deficit-elimination process. In the three-year budget agreement concluded between President Bush and the Democratic-led Congress in 1990 (the "Andrews Air Force Base Agreement"), the international affairs function as well as the national defense function of the budget was fenced off and protected from diversion to alternative spending. By contrast, at the conclusion of the January 1996 budget negotiations, there was political agreement to put a floor under the national defense budget, but international affairs was grouped with all other nondefense discretionary expenditures and targeted by the Office of Management and Budget (OMB) for straight-line reductions. Subsequent pleas from the State Department for the protection of foreign affairs within a more expansive "national security" category were of no avail.

CONSEQUENCES

THE STATE DEPARTMENT and its 260-plus overseas posts constitute the basic and indispensable infrastructure upon which all U.S. civilian—and many military—elements rely to protect and promote American interests around the world. The Task Force found unmistakable evidence that the readiness of this infrastructure has been seriously eroded. Some 30 posts have been closed in the past three years for lack of operating funds. Many of the remaining posts

---

[4] The out-year projections in the president's proposed budget for fiscal year 1998, released after this Statement was completed, contemplate spending of $16.8 billion in fiscal year 2002 (expressed in constant 1997 dollars).

are shabby, unsafe, and ill-equipped. All are handicapped by obsolete information technology. Staffing is highly uneven. The department's cadre of language and area specialists has been depleted and resources for public diplomacy are fast disappearing. Yet the demands upon our missions continue to grow. Reports circulate that budget cuts may force the department to close more posts abroad and that the department is being advised to sell off its assets in order to meet operating expenses. Taken together, these developments contribute to an image of decline and withdrawal that disheartens our friends and allies and undermines our effectiveness abroad, as do the actual cuts in our diplomatic muscle.

More subtle is the extent to which the executive's options have been severely limited for lack of readily available, flexible resources with which to avert or respond to foreign crises. Future chief executives, regardless of party, will find this every bit as vexing as has the present incumbent.

In the recent past our government has been forced to choose, sometimes arbitrarily, which situations it will engage in and which it will ignore. Here are some recent examples:

- To stabilize Haiti, the decision had to be made to reduce economic support for Turkey, despite its critical relationship to our Middle East interests.
- The decision to provide aid to shore up the West Bank and Gaza was made at the expense of funds originally intended to help demobilize the armed forces of the parties to a Central American peace agreement that the United States had spent years negotiating.
- Providing our share of the financing package assembled for Cambodia's first free election required deferring, for more than a year, support for smaller initiatives in a dozen or so other countries.
- Responding to the refugee crisis in Rwanda meant taking funds for democratic institution-building from the rest of Africa at a moment when positive trends were emerging elsewhere on the continent.
- When the United States needed $2 million to monitor a ceasefire between the Kurdish factions in northern Iraq, ready money

was not immediately available, the situation deteriorated, and Saddam Hussein was afforded a pretext to send forces into northern Iraq—a move that culminated in U.S. military action costing multiples of the originally needed sum.

U.S. investment in economic development, either through our bilateral programs or international financial institutions (IFIs) like the World Bank, has declined to $9 billion from the $12 billion average of the earlier 1990s. It is projected to fall every year under both the president's and the congressional out-year plans. The consequences of not investing in development are impossible to quantify, but the evidence of the benefits that development has brought to over one-half of the world's population is impressive. In the purely human dimension, U.S. bilateral leadership has been critical to recent worldwide advances in agricultural and medical research and basic human needs including primary education, family planning, child nutrition, and immunization programs.

U.S. political and economic self-interest also benefits from the activities of the IFIs. But as we fall behind in meeting our commitments, we risk losing our ability to shape their agendas in support of our objectives. In the past, this influence has enabled us to mobilize multilateral funding to supplement our own increasingly limited bilateral funds for reconstruction in Bosnia, Haiti, and the West Bank/Gaza; to stabilize the Mexican peso; and to reinforce the transitions to democracy in Central Europe and the countries of the former Soviet Union. At home, U.S. exporters expect to feel the effects if our support for the IFIs continues to decline. Nearly one-half of U.S. exports go to Asia, Latin America, and Africa, where close to 80 percent of the world's population lives. IFI lending drives critical segments of development that, in turn, will determine the future market potential of these countries.

U.S. arrearages to the United Nations present a more complicated and troublesome case. An independent Council on Foreign Relations–sponsored Task Force chaired by George Soros recently concluded that when the United States had taken clear and firm positions, the United Nations "has served U.S. interests well." The report noted further that its judgments of the United Nations' utility "have been shared by both the Bush and Clinton administrations." But the United Nations will not continue to work for us, particularly after we succeeded in imposing our will on the issue of a new secretary general, if we are not prepared to meet our financial obligations. Nor will our efforts toward reform of the U.N. system gain momentum if it appears that the United States is unlikely to settle its arrearages, which now amount to $300 million for the regular budget and $700 million for peacekeeping operations.

The damaging implications of the planned, progressive reduction in the international affairs budget are immediately evident upon examination of the limited options for their implementation. The most obvious strategy would be to take most of the cut out of one or the other of its largest components—development assistance and the Israel/Egypt programs. Either could be virtually eliminated if it were targeted. The alternative would be to cut each component proportionately. Under this scenario, the State Department could not avoid closing nearly 100 additional posts, and funding for "new global issues"—including crime, corruption, narcotics, and the environment—would be at risk.

The magnitude of the cuts proposed through the year 2002 would make it impossible to avoid significant cuts in support of the Middle East peace process and development aid, regardless of the strength and persuasiveness of their advocates within the U.S. political process. Those programs are where the money is, and if total cuts of a cumulative magnitude of nearly 50 percent are made, they simply cannot be spared.

Advocates of sharp reductions in international spending frequently do not spell out how their recommendations should be implemented. They may be prepared to see one activity or another savaged but would probably find at least one of the above-mentioned consequences of drastic cuts unacceptable.

None of this is meant to imply that there is no room for selective reductions in foreign aid or no need for a tighter focus on administering its distribution. Insufficient funding is by no means the only problem with our foreign affairs programs. However, any changes should be made with a scalpel rather than an ax. The Task Force has identified several specific areas where savings could be made in order to enhance effectiveness and to offset partially the increases it proposes.

RECOMMENDATIONS

TO REVERSE the destructive funding trend of the last few years, the president must take the initiative to ask for adequate funding for international affairs and to work together with Congress to ensure that our foreign affairs structure is organized to meet today's requirements with maximum efficiency and effectiveness. He must take responsibility for doing what only he can do—explain to the American people why we need to devote resources to promoting our interests abroad. At the same time, he must make clear to the foreign affairs bureaucracy that "business as usual" is unacceptable. All the poll data show that the American people support constructive engagement and recognize the dangers and opportunities abroad. They know leadership does not come cheap and they will support the president once he makes clear what is needed and that he is prepared to push for reform.[5]

Next, the executive and Congress must reestablish the bipartisan and bicameral cooperation necessary to ensure that adequate funds are provided. Otherwise, American interests will be increasingly at risk in a rapidly changing and turbulent world. To the extent that agreement can be reached between the president and Congress on restructuring the foreign affairs agencies, it would be highly desirable to agree on basic terms in time for any necessary legislative action to be completed during the coming session of Congress.

Specifically, in FY 1998, federal discretionary spending on international affairs should rise to $21 billion from its 1997 level of $19 billion, with annual adjustments through the year 2002 to offset infla-

---

[5] Bowman Cutter emphasizes that in the current budget climate this recommendation necessarily involves shifting $2 billion annually away from other, presumably domestic programs, and that this policy thrust carries with it a heavy responsibility on the part of policymakers to examine thoroughly the structure and operational effectiveness of our current programs.

tion. The recommended figure is still well below the average of the 1980–95 time period but considerably more than current projections.

The Task Force was acutely aware of the continuing budget pressures and searched for ways to cut existing costs. The Task Force presents these reforms before outlining the increases that are recommended:

- Savings in the development assistance account can be realized by dropping the Title I PL 480 food program and through the amalgamation of the Agency for International Development's extensive administrative support operations as discussed below.[6]
- Continuing administrative reforms in U.N. organizations and the international financial organizations should produce savings for the U.S. expenditures on the United Nations of $100 million per year by the year 2002.
- Amalgamation and reengineering of the administrative support services of the foreign affairs agencies need not await the larger structural review recommended and therefore should be initiated immediately. This reform would be a logical follow-on to the newly agreed-upon collaborative arrangements for financing overseas administrative support. The foreign affairs agencies should be directed to move without further delay to eliminate overlap and duplication of policy and program functions among themselves, as directed by the vice president in 1995. These actions should produce savings of $100 million to $200 million by the end of the decade.
- A mission-by-mission review of all agencies' overseas staffing should be considered as a means of sharpening focus and realigning resources with policy priorities. Such a review could achieve additional savings in accounts other than 150.

---

[6] Julia V. Taft would like to point out that in recent years an important portion of the tonnage allotted to Title I has been reprogrammed for emergency food response under Title II and has contributed to major life-saving programs. If the budget is saved by dropping Title I, it will not really save money if there needs to be a complicated, supplemental food allocation for highly popular humanitarian food aid under Title II. For this reason, she questions the validity of the cost savings and wonders if we might be jeopardizing the support of the U.S. farmers who strongly support PL 480.

Statement of the Task Force

The Task Force is persuaded that some restructuring of the foreign affairs agencies is needed and that this would produce additional savings—although less than some advocates have suggested. Restructuring the foreign affairs agencies is a task assigned by the Constitution and by practical necessity to both political branches of the government and requires the cooperation of leaders on both ends of Pennsylvania Avenue. The Task Force urges the president and congressional leaders to come together on a mechanism—a bipartisan commission appointed jointly by congressional leaders and the president is one time-honored method—to develop a solution that all can support and that will improve the formation and implementation of policy.

Disagreement over organization must not be permitted to be the cause or the excuse for failure to reach agreement on the funding increases that will be necessary—whatever structural reforms are agreed upon. The following summarizes the Task Force's recommendations for increases relative to FY 1997 spending levels (all numbers are annual unless otherwise indicated, should be maintained at this level in real terms for the next five years, and are expressed in constant 1997 dollars):

- $600 million should be available in accounts that the president can draw upon to take prompt, concrete actions to fix problems of urgent and particular concern to the United States. Uses would include economic and security support, military education and training, foreign military financing, conflict prevention and resolution, democratic institution-building, nonproliferation, counternarcotics, and counterterrorism. These are basic tools of U.S. policy that any president will require. The ability to package them quickly can often give the United States critical leverage in dealing with impending crises, particularly where unilateral American interests are at stake or where, for whatever reason, resources from other governments or multilateral institutions are either not available or cannot be mobilized without U.S. participation. Use of these funds should be permitted on a discretionary basis, subject to strict accountability to Congress.
- The basic State Department operating accounts should be

maintained at least at the FY 1997 level in real terms until FY 2002. In addition, two temporary increases are recommended:

1. A "no year" capital investment account should be created for information technology modernization tied to State's Information Resource Management Strategic Plan funded at $150 million annually for five years. The modernized systems would support not only the State Department but also the 40-plus other U.S. agencies housed in U.S. posts abroad, permitting (for the first time) modern communication among agencies at post and facilitating the consolidation of administrative support systems. The State Department's requirements for the replacement and repair of overall plant and equipment substantially exceed this amount, but the Task Force expects these to be met through reinvestment of savings generated by reengineering of State's Washington-based overhead functions.

2. A two-year "Reorganization Account" funded at $100 million annually to be administered by the State Department under special authorities to facilitate (e.g., through retraining, outplacement, "early-out" retirements, lease terminations, etc.) the consolidation and downsizing of administrative overhead and duplicative program functions among the foreign affairs agencies. From FY 2000 on, savings generated by this restructuring should kick in, permitting the recovery of transition costs and generating on-going savings to help offset planned inflation adjustments.

- $200 million should be budgeted annually for five years to eliminate approximately $1 billion in U.S. arrears to the United Nations, pursuant to executive-congressional agreement on much-needed U.N. reforms.

- A $500-million net increase in bilateral support for sustainable development and poverty eradication, disbursed primarily through the Agency for International Development (AID), would begin to move funding for those activities back toward the average of the earlier 1990s. At the same time, AID should give consideration to tightening still further the practice that it has begun of reducing or eliminating programs when recipient governments do not pursue policies consistent with sustainable growth.

• $700 million (in increased budget authority) should go in increased budget authority to the international financial institutions (IFIs). Within this total, $200 million for five years would make good on arrears, together with an annual increase of $500 million for replenishment in capitalization of multilateral banks and funding of the International Development Association. As the terms of future capitalizations are considered, the United States should insist that IFIs require recipient governments to adhere to growth-compatible economic policies.[7, 8]

CONCLUSION

THE PRESIDENT has spoken very clearly about the imperatives of global leadership and its price. In Detroit last October he declared:

> The burden of American leadership and the importance of it—indeed, the essential character of American leadership—is one of the great lessons of the 20th century. It will be an even more powerful reality in the 21st century.

What remains now is for the president to recognize that without adequate resources it will not be possible to provide the international leadership that our national interests require. There are three aspects to this challenge:

---

[7] David Abshire would like to note that the extent to which the multilateral development banks (MDBs) should change their focus to take account of recent changes, especially the huge expansion of private flows, and reforms needed to improve their effectiveness are the subject of a forthcoming Center for Strategic and International Studies Task Force (CSIS) report. Chaired by Senator Bill Bradley and Congressman John Kasich, this Task Force will recommend tighter MDB policies on country graduation, policy reform, and competition with the private sector. It also stresses the need for more transparency in MDB operations and a better system by which shareholders can judge program results. According to Abshire, this group believes U.S. funding for the MDBs should be related to progress in these areas, but still under discussion is the time frame over which reforms should be expected.

[8] Steven K. Berry concurs with the CSIS Task Force's preliminary findings, noted by David Abshire above, regarding restructuring and focusing multilateral development bank energies on economically viable projects.

First, the president must include in his 1998 budget request an amount adequate to fund American leadership, and he must also reverse the out-year projections that threaten our posture abroad. Second, the president must take the international affairs resource issue to the American people. The president, more than any other individual or institution in our system, bears the responsibility for the success or failure of American foreign policy. Better than anyone else, he can make clear what it means not to have the resources required to protect and promote American values and interests. As commander in chief, the president can underscore the vital link between diplomacy and deterrence. Then-Secretary of State Warren Christopher described the nature of this connection very clearly when he addressed the Corps of Cadets at West Point last October 25:

> We will serve the American people best of all if we can prevent the conflicts and emergencies that call for a military response from ever arising . . . if we hold that line around the world, we are much less likely to have to send you and the troops you will command into harm's way sometime in the future.

Third, once the president has done these two things he will be in a position to reach out to the leadership of Congress to establish an understanding about international affairs financing. This must be a collaborative, nonpartisan undertaking, and the president must commit, at the outset, to a review of the structure and coordination of the foreign policy agencies as recommended above. The initial move in this regard must be the president's, and it must be accompanied by a clear indication of his willingness to take the resource issue to the American people. He must then be joined by Congress, which deserves nothing less than a full understanding, a full voice in decisions, and a full measure of responsibility.

The American people do not want to swap a budget deficit for a security deficit. The Task Force suspects most Americans would be alarmed if these proposed budget cuts go through and they then discover that America faces an influence gap in world affairs as we enter the 21st century.

We can afford to do more. We cannot afford to do less.

Endorsers of the Statement

Signatories include members of the Task Force, regional participants who met in Boston and Seattle, and those who have since endorsed the Task Force Statement.

DAVID M. ABSHIRE cofounded the Center for Strategic and International Studies in 1962 and currently serves as its President and Chief Executive Officer. A graduate of West Point, he served as U.S. Ambassador to NATO from 1983 to 1987 and as Special Counselor to the President in 1987. He is the author of five books, including *Preventing World War III* and *Putting America's House in Order: The Nation as a Family* (with Brock Bower).

CLARK C. ABT is Chairman of Abt Associates, Inc., an international economic research and consulting firm. He was Professor of International Relations at Boston University and Director of the four Russian-American Entrepreneurial Workshops in Defense Technology Conversion for nuclear weapons scientists.

GRAHAM T. ALLISON, JR., is Director of Harvard University's Center for Science and International Affairs and the Douglas Dillon Professor of Government. He previously served as Assistant Secretary of Defense for Policy and Planning.

ROBERT J. ART is Herter Professor of International Relations at Brandeis University and Research Associate at the Olin Institute for Strategic Studies, Harvard University.

ROBERT L. BARRY is a Partner in Phoenix International, an electric power development company, and a Senior Associate of the Center for Strategic and International Studies. During his Foreign Service career, he was Ambassador to Indonesia, Bulgaria, and the Stockholm Conference on Security.

[15]

STEVEN K. BERRY is a Partner at Holland & Knight. He served as Chief Counsel to the Senate Foreign Relations Committee from 1993 to 1996, Deputy and Acting Assistant Secretary of State for Legislative Affairs from 1990 to 1993, and Chief of Staff on the House Foreign Affairs Committee from 1986 to 1990.

DEREK BOK is 300th Anniversary University Professor at Harvard University and served as Harvard's President from 1971 to 1991.

SALIH BOOKER is the Senior Fellow for Africa Studies at the Council on Foreign Relations. He was a professional staff member of the House Foreign Affairs Committee and served in Africa as a program officer for the Ford Foundation.

TERRENCE L. BRACY is Chairman of Bracy Williams and Company and is an organizer of the Business Alliance for International Economic Development. He served as Assistant Secretary of Transportation and currently chairs the Morris K. Udall Foundation.

ZBIGNIEW BRZEZINSKI is Counselor at the Center for Strategic and Advanced International Studies and Professor of American Foreign Policy at the School of Advanced International Studies, the Johns Hopkins University. From 1977 to 1981, he was National Security Advisor to the President of the United States and in 1981 he was awarded the Presidential Medal of Freedom for his role in the normalization of U.S.-Chinese relations and for his contributions to the human rights and national security policies of the United States.

JOHN A. BURGESS is a Senior Partner in the Boston, Massachusetts, law firm of Hale and Dorr. He is Co-Chair of the firm's Corporate Department and Chair of its International Practice Group.

MARK BURNS is an officer in the U.S. Air Force and is currently pursuing a degree at the John F. Kennedy School of Government at Harvard University.

GEORGE BURRILL is Chairperson of the Business Alliance for International Economic Development as well as founder of ARD Inc., an international consulting firm. He is an expert in international development issues.

RICHARD R. BURT is Chairman of International Equity Partners Advisors. He served as Ambassador to West Germany from 1985 to 1989 and as Assistant Secretary of State for Europe from 1983 to 1989.

JOHN C. CAMPBELL is Senior Fellow, Emeritus, at the Council on Foreign Relations. He is a former Director of Studies at the Council and served on the Policy Planning Staff of the State Department.

FRANK C. CARLUCCI is Chairman of the Carlyle Group, a Washington, D.C.–based merchant bank. He is a former Secretary of Defense, National Security Advisor, and Foreign Service Officer.

CHARLES E. COBB, JR., is Chairman of the Board of the Pan Am Corporation. He served as Ambassador to Iceland during the Bush administration and as Undersecretary and Assistant Secretary at the Commerce Department during the Reagan administration.

W. BOWMAN CUTTER is a Managing Director of the venture capital firm of Warburg, Pincus in New York City. Immediately prior to joining Warburg, Pincus, he served in the National Economic Council as Deputy Assistant to the President for Economic Policy.

PATRICIA DAVIS is President of the Washington Council on International Trade, an association of private sector interests working to support policies favorable to expanded trade. She is also an elected member of the Seattle Port Commission, which manages harbor facilities and the Seattle-Tacoma International Airport.

BREWSTER C. DENNY is Professor and Dean Emeritus, University of Washington, Seattle, where he teaches American Diplomatic History. He is a Trustee and former Chairman (1986–94) of the Twentieth Century Fund, has served as U.S. Representative to the United Nations, and was on the staff of Senator Henry M. Jackson's Subcommittee on National Policy Machinery.

MARK D.W. EDINGTON is an Editor of *Daedalus,* the journal of the American Academy of Arts and Sciences, and Director of the Boston Committee on Foreign Relations.

MICKEY EDWARDS is a Lecturer in Public Policy at the John F. Kennedy School of Government at Harvard University. Prior to joining the Harvard faculty, he served 16 years as a Congressman from Oklahoma and was Chairman of the House Republican Policy Committee, the fourth-ranking Republican leadership position in the House of Representatives.

ROBERT F. ELLSWORTH is the Managing Director of the Hamilton Group LLC and Senior Partner of the Deane Group. He served as former Assistant and Deputy Secretary of Defense from 1974 to 1977, and as Ambassador to NATO from 1969 to 1971.

AINSLIE T. EMBREE is Professor Emeritus of History at Columbia University, where he was Associate Dean of the School of International and Public Affairs. He was Cultural Counselor at the American Embassy in New Delhi and later Special Consultant to Ambassador Frank Wisner.

DANTE B. FASCELL is with Holland & Knight. He served in Congress for 38 years and from 1983 to 1992 was Chair of the House Foreign Affairs Committee.

RICHARD A. FALKENRATH is Executive Director of the Center for Science and International Affairs, Harvard University.

RICHARD W. FISHER is Managing Partner of Fisher Capital Management and Adjunct Professor of Public Management at the University of Texas. He was the Democratic nominee for the U.S. Senate in 1994 and is Founding Chairman of the Dallas Committee on Foreign Relations.

BART FRIEDMAN is a Senior Partner of Cahill Gordon & Reindel. An active member of both the Council on Foreign Relations and the Council of the Brookings Institution, he also serves as Vice Chairman of the Juilliard School in New York and as a member of the Visiting Committee to Harvard University's Graduate School of Education.

JEFFREY E. GARTEN is Dean of the Yale School of Management. He was Under Secretary of Commerce for International Trade from 1993 to 1995 and was formerly a Managing Director of the Blackstone Group.

WILLIAM E. GRIFFITH is Ford Professor of Political Science, Emeritus, at the Massachusetts Institute of Technology. He was Minister Counselor at the United States Embassy, Bonn, from 1985 to 1986.

ADAM R. GRISSOM is a master's candidate at Harvard University's John F. Kennedy School of Government. In recent years he has been an adviser to UNPROFOR and studied NATO communications programs for the U.S. Army.

PETER GROSE is a Research Fellow at the Center for Science and International Affairs, Harvard University. He is the author of books on U.S.-Israel relations and American intelligence and was Executive Editor of *Foreign Affairs.*

RICHARD N. HAASS is Director of Foreign Policy Studies at the Brookings Institution. He served as Special Assistant to President Bush and Senior Director for Near East and South Asian Affairs at the National Security Council.

ALEXANDER M. HAIG, JR. (General U.S. Army, Retired), is Chairman of Worldwide Associates, Inc. He served as Secretary of State (1981–82), Supreme Allied Commander, Europe (1974–79), and White House Chief of Staff (1973–74).

MORTON H. HALPERIN is a Senior Fellow of the Council on Foreign Relations. He served in the Defense Department during the Johnson and Clinton administrations and on the staff of the National Security Council during the Nixon and Clinton administrations.

WILLIAM C. HARROP is a Director of the Barista Coffee Company, the Association for Diplomatic Studies and Training, and the American Academy of Diplomacy. He was Ambassador to Israel, Zaire, Kenya, Seychelles, and Guinea and served as Inspector General of the State Department and Foreign Service.

ALAN K. HENRIKSON is Director of the Fletcher Roundtable on a New World Order at the Fletcher School of Law and Diplomacy, Tufts University. He is also an Affiliate of the Center for International Affairs at Harvard University.

JESSICA HOBART is a graduate of Swarthmore College and the John F. Kennedy School of Government. She is currently working at the Center for Science and International Affairs at Harvard University.

CELES ECKERMAN HUGHES is a student of international security policy at the John F. Kennedy School of Government. She worked previously on national security and arms control issues for Senator Edward M. Kennedy, the Arms Control Association, and the Henry L. Stimson Center.

PATRICIA L. IRVIN is the Managing Partner of the Washington, D.C., office of Cooper, Liebowitz, Royster & Wright. She served as Deputy Assistant Secretary of Defense for Humanitarian Affairs and was a Partner in the Wall Street law firm Milbank, Tweed, Hadley & McCloy.

PAULA C. JACOBSON is a graduate of Yale College and the John F. Kennedy School of Government. Before coming to Harvard, she served on the foreign policy legislative staff of Senator Daniel Patrick Moynihan.

KEMPTON B. JENKINS is Executive Director of the Ukraine-U.S. Business Council. He served as Principal Deputy Assistant Secretary of State for Congressional Relations, Deputy Assistant Secretary of State for East-West Trade, and Assistant Director of USIA for the U.S.S.R. and Eastern Europe during his 32-year diplomatic career.

WILLARD R. JOHNSON has been a member of the Massachusetts Institute of Technology Political Science Department since 1964. He is a member of the Council on Foreign Relations, was a founder of TransAfrica, and has been a leader in several organizations concerned with promoting democracy, development, and respect for human rights.

MAX M. KAMPELMAN is President of the American Academy of Diplomacy, Chairman of the Georgetown University Institute for the Study of Diplomacy, and Vice Chairman of the U.S. Institute of Peace. He was Ambassador and Head of Delegation to the Negotiations on Nuclear and Space Arms and to the Conference on Security and Cooperation in Europe.

ARNOLD KANTER is a Senior Associate at the Forum for International Policy. He has served as Undersecretary of State for Political Affairs and as Special Assistant to the President for Defense Policy and Arms Control.

LANE KIRKLAND worked for the AFL-CIO from 1948 until 1995 and served as its President from 1976 to 1995.

LAWRENCE J. KORB is currently the Director of the Center for Public Policy Education at the Brookings Institution. He served as Assistant Secretary of Defense for Manpower Installations and Logistics throughout the first and into the second Reagan administrations.

CAROL J. LANCASTER is on the faculty of the School of Foreign Service of Georgetown University and is a Visiting Fellow at the Institute for International Economics. She has served in the State

Department and the Agency for International Development, most recently as Deputy Administrator of AID (1993–96).

SALLY LILIENTHAL is Founder and President of the Ploughshares Fund and former Vice President of Amnesty International, U.S.A.

FRANKLIN A. LINDSAY is the retired Chairman of Itek Corporation and former Chairman of the National Bureau for Economic Research. He was assistant to Averell Harriman, head of the Marshall Plan organization in Paris, and Secretary of the U.S. Delegation to the U.N. Atomic Energy Commission.

SARAH K. LISCHER is a graduate student in International Security at Harvard University. She has directed a refugee resettlement agency and taught at a South African high school.

MATTHEW F. MCHUGH is Counselor to the President of the World Bank. He represented New York in the U.S. House of Representatives from 1975 to 1992, serving on the Foreign Aid Subcommittee of the Appropriations Committee.

M. PETER MCPHERSON is President of Michigan State University. He served as Administrator, AID (seven years), Deputy Secretary of the Treasury Department (two years), and Group Executive Vice President at the Bank of America.

DAVID C. MEADE, Major General U.S. Army (Retired), was the Commander of the 10th Mountain Division and Commander of the U.S. Joint Task Force and Multinational Forces in Haiti. Among other senior positions, he has served as Director, Army Strategy and Planning.

ROBERT F. MEAGHER is a Consultant on International Economic Law, Legal Advisor to the India Interest Group, and Emeritus Professor of International Law at the Fletcher School of Law and Diplomacy, Tufts University.

ROBERT H. MICHEL is Senior Advisor for Corporate and Governmental Affairs at Hogan & Hartson. He joined the firm in 1995 after serving 38 years in Congress as the U.S. Representative from the 18th Congressional District in Illinois, including 14 years as House Minority Leader.

RICHARD M. MOOSE served as Under Secretary for Management at the State Department from 1993 to 1996. Previously he was a Senior Vice President at the American Express Company, a Managing Director of Shearson Lehman Brothers, and Assistant Secretary for African Affairs (1978–81), and he has held positions on the National Security Council and the Senate Foreign Relations Committee.

KENNETH P. MORSE is currently Managing Director of the MIT Entrepreneurship Center. He founded five high-tech companies, all of which were highly successful in the international arena.

JOSHUA MURAVCHIK is a resident scholar at the American Enterprise Institute. He is the author of many articles and several books, including *The Imperative of American Leadership, Exporting Democracy,* and *The Uncertain Crusade.*

TED M. NATT is Editor and Publisher of the *Daily News* in Longview, Washington. He led his newspaper to the Pulitzer Prize in 1981.

DAVID NEMTZOW is President of the Alliance to Save Energy, a nonprofit coalition of government, industry, consumer, and environmental leaders dedicated to promoting greater investment in energy and efficiency. He is a member of the Board of Directors of the Alliance and Chairman of the Export Council for Energy Efficiency.

RICHARD A. NENNEMAN was Managing Editor and Editor-in-Chief of the *Christian Science Monitor* from 1983 to 1993. He has served as Chairman of the Boston Committee on Foreign Relations and is a member of the Council on Foreign Relations and the American Council on Germany.

AUGUSTUS RICHARD NORTON is Professor of Anthropology and International Relations at Boston University. He was Professor of Political Science at the U.S. Military Academy and has been a recipient of major foreign affairs grants from the MacArthur and Ford Foundations.

JOSEPH S. NYE, JR., is Dean of the John F. Kennedy School of Government at Harvard University and former Assistant Secretary of Defense for International Security Affairs.

GORDON W. PERKIN, M.D., is President of Path Program for Appropriate Technology in Health, a nonprofit Seattle-based organization whose mission is to improve the health of women and children in developing countries.

RICHARD E. PIPES is Professor of History, Emeritus, Harvard University. He served as Director of East European and Soviet Affairs at the National Security Council and is the author of *The Russian Revolution.*

BRENT SCOWCROFT is President of the Forum for International Policy, a nonprofit organization that advocates American leadership in foreign policy. He was the National Security Advisor to President Bush from 1989 to 1993.

SARAH B. SEWALL is an International Affairs Fellow at the Program on Negotiation at Harvard. She was Deputy Assistant Secretary of Defense for Peacekeeping and Humanitarian Affairs and served as Senate Majority Leader George Mitchell's Senior Foreign Policy Advisor.

JOHN W. SEWELL is President of the Overseas Development Council (ODC), an international policy research institute that seeks to inform and improve multilateral approaches and institutions that promote development and the management of related global problems. Prior to joining ODC, he worked at the Brookings Institution and served in the U.S. Foreign Service.

GEORGE P. SHULTZ served as U.S. Secretary of State from 1982 to 1989. He is currently a Distinguished Fellow at the Hoover Institution and Professor at Stanford University.

EUGENE B. SKOLNIKOFF is a Professor of Political Science at the Massachusetts Institute of Technology. He has written widely on science, technology, and international affairs and served in the White House during several administrations in the office of Special Assistant to the President for Science and Technology.

STEPHEN J. SOLARZ is a Senior Counselor at APCO Associates, the Director of the George Washington University Foreign Policy Forum, and a member of the Board of the National Endowment for Democracy as well as several private sector boards. Congressman Solarz (D-NY) served as Chairman of the House Foreign Affairs Subcommittee on Asian and Pacific Affairs and the Subcommittee on Africa during his service from 1975 to 1992 in the House of Representatives.

THEODORE C. SORENSEN is with Paul, Weiss, and Rifkind Wharton & Garrison in New York. Previously he served as Assistant to Senator John F. Kennedy (1953–61) and Special Counsel to Presidents Kennedy and Johnson (1961–64).

CLAUDE A. SOUDAH is Senior Vice President and Manager of the International Operations Division at Seafirst Bank. Active in international banking for 31 years, he is Director of the Executive Committee of the Washington Council on International Trade.

DEBORAH L. SPAR is Associate Professor at Harvard Business School.

JULIA V. TAFT is President and CEO of InterAction, a coalition of over 150 U.S.-based relief and development agencies. She previously was Director of the Agency for International Development Office of Foreign Disaster Assistance and the Coordinator for Refugees in the State Department.

DICK THORNBURGH is Counsel to the law firm of Kirkpatrick & Lockhart LLP, Washington, D.C. He served as Under Secretary General of the United Nations (1978–79), Attorney General of the United States (1988–91), and Governor of Pennsylvania.

ROBERT J.C. VAN LEEUWEN is Executive Director of the World Affairs Council in Seattle. He was Deputy Representative of the United Nations High Commissioner for Refugees (UNHCR) in Thailand when the office was awarded the Nobel Peace Prize. He later served as UNHCR Chief of Mission in Hong Kong and Pakistan.

ABELARDO LOPEZ VALDEZ currently practices international law in Washington, D.C. He served as Chief of Protocol of the United States (1979–91); Assistant Administrator for Latin America, Agency for International Development (1977–79); General Counsel, InterAmerican Foundation (1973–75); and Attorney for the U.S. Overseas Private Investment Corporation (1973–75).

CYRUS R. VANCE is a Senior Partner at Simpson Thatcher & Bartlett and has held numerous positions in the State and Defense Departments. He served as Secretary of State from 1977 to 1980.

PAUL A. VOLCKER recently retired as Chairman and Chief Executive officer of Wolfensohn & Co., Inc. upon the merger of that firm with Bankers Trust, of which he will become a Director. Previously, he was Chairman of the Board of Governors of the Federal Reserve System from 1979 to 1987 and President of the Federal Reserve Bank of New York from 1975 to 1979.

RAYMOND J. WALDMANN is Vice President, International Business, for the Boeing Company. He serves on and formerly chaired the U.S. government's Aerospace Industry Sector Committee and has held several senior positions in government. He was a member of the White House staff under Presidents Nixon and Ford.

LOUIS T. WELLS is the Herbert F. Johnson Professor of International Management at Harvard Business School.

JENNIFER SEYMOUR WHITAKER is Deputy National Director and Senior Fellow at the Council on Foreign Relations. She was formerly Co-Director of the Committee on African Development

Strategies and is the author of *How Can Africa Survive?* and *Salvaging the Land of Plenty.*

JOHN C. WHITEHEAD is Chairman of the Federal Reserve Bank of New York and of the United Nations Association of the United States. He is the former Chairman of Goldman, Sachs and Co. and was Deputy Secretary of State from 1985 to 1989.

EDEN Y. WOON is Executive Director of the Washington State China Relations Council, a nonprofit organization with over 178 members who do business in China. He was the China Policy Advisor to the Secretary of Defense.

DOROTHY S. ZINBERG is a Lecturer on Public Policy at the John F. Kennedy School of Government's Center for Science and International Affairs.

JEREMY ZUCKER currently attends the John F. Kennedy School of Government at Harvard University. He is a graduate of Yale University and has worked on Wall Street in Latin American finance.

Background Materials

BACKGROUND STUDY

Prepared by Michael O'Hanlon

RELATIVE TO THE AVERAGE of the 1980s, spending on international affairs has fallen nearly 20 percent in real terms, and it could decline by as much as another 30 percent under the plans of the president and Congress for balancing the federal budget.

It was appropriate that certain international affairs accounts decline from their Cold War levels. Security aid no longer needs to be as large as when the Western world faced a global Communist threat. Further economies in remaining accounts may be possible as well. Certain programs, such as the non–disaster-related parts of the PL 480 food aid program, are inefficient or even counterproductive. The U.N. Secretariat in New York is not well managed. Too much development aid still flows to countries with poor macroeconomic policies; many such countries should receive less assistance than they currently do.

But on balance, it appears clear that the ability of the United States to promote its interests and values on a global scale has already been jeopardized—if not significantly harmed—as a result of excessive budget cuts. Unless these trends are reversed, the consequences for U.S. interests around the world could be dire.

For those who would downplay the stakes involved, a quick survey of this century's chief historical turning points should give them pause. U.S. disengagement from the international scene after World War I helped pave the way for World War II. U.S. engagement after World War II helped create and hold together the most successful alliance system in world history, the alliance that eventually prevailed in the Cold War. Although fear of a common threat helped create and coalesce the U.S.-centered Western alliance network, common values and an energetic and generous U.S. leadership also contributed greatly. Most countries trusted the United States and believed it would act to promote not just its own but general international interests.

With the century's third and final great geopolitical contest now over, how the United States sets up the machinery and priorities of future foreign policy will have great bearing on the likelihood of war, peace, and prosperity in the next century. If its positive vision for a harmonious and prosperous community of nations becomes clouded, the values espoused by leaders from Roosevelt to Reagan will lose their greatest champion and almost certainly be weakened on the global scene.

Senator Richard Lugar, Republican of Indiana, put it well. In a recent admonition to the country's policymakers, he said:

> Too many leaders in both political parties have bowed to political expedience and embraced the fiction that international spending does not benefit Americans and therefore can be cut with impunity. As important as balancing the budget is, it will not happen if American disengagement from the world results in nuclear terrorism, an international trade war, an international energy crisis, a major regional conflict requiring U.S. intervention, or some other preventable disaster that undermines our security and prosperity.[1]

As much as other countries can threaten our interests, they can also benefit our economy, strengthen our diplomacy, and enrich our lives. Exports and imports combined now represent one-quarter of the U.S. gross domestic product (GDP); 10 million more Americans a year now travel overseas than a decade ago; coordinated multilateral efforts to protect the environment or address financial and political crises in countries like Russia and Mexico can succeed more readily, and at much lower cost to American taxpayers, than unilateral U.S. efforts.

Clearly, general arguments like the above do not immediately translate into a specific international affairs budget. But it now appears that the United States has reached the point where cutbacks have

---

[1] Quoted in Helen Dewar, "Sen. Lugar Rules Out State Dept. Possibility," *Washington Post,* November 9, 1996, p. A4.

indeed begun to interfere with the effective implementation of American foreign policy.

In 1997, the United States will spend about $19.6 billion for its major diplomatic and foreign assistance activities. That amount is slightly more than one percent of the overall federal budget (see figure 1). It is less in real or inflation-adjusted terms than international discretionary spending in any year since 1979 (excepting 1996) and nearly 20 percent below the average amount since then.

International affairs is the only major category of federal spending that has been reduced in real terms since 1980 (see table 1). Moreover, international spending is one of only two major components of the federal budget that have been reduced in real terms since 1990. Military spending has also declined since then, but that was to be expected with the collapse of the Soviet military machine.

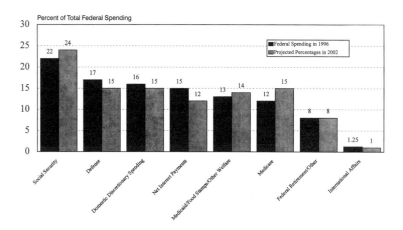

Figure 1. U.S. Federal Spending by Category, 1996 and 2002
(projections based on the president's budget)
Sources: Congressional Budget Office, *Economic and Budget Outlook: Fiscal Years 1997–2006* (May 1996); Executive Office of the President, *Budget of the United States Government, Fiscal Year 1998, Historical Tables* (February 1997), p. 109.
Note: These percentages add up to roughly 104; offsetting receipts (negative spending) bring the actual total back down to 100 percent.
   "Federal Retirement" includes military pensions; "other" includes unemployment compensation. The "Medicaid/Food Stamps/Other Welfare" category includes the earned income tax credit. Each percent of current federal spending represents about $15 billion. The "projected percentages" show spending estimates for 2020 under the president's long-term budget.

Table 1. The Federal Budget, 1962–2002
(outlays, constant 1997 $billion)

Type of Spending	1962	1980	1990	Pres. 1997	Pres. 2002	Change '80–97	Change '90–97	Change '90–02
International Discretionary	26 (5)	24 (2)	23 (1.5)	19.6 (1.2)	17 (1)	-18%	-15%	-26%
National Defense Discretionary	248 (49)	251 (23)	358 (24)	268 (16)	242 (15)	+7%	-25%	-32%
Domestic Discretionary	64 (13)	240 (22)	216 (14)	263 (16)	242 (15)	+10%	+22%	+12%
Social Security	66 (13)	217 (20)	294 (20)	364 (22)	407 (24)	+68%	+24%	+38%
Medicaid, Other Means-Tested Entitlements	20 (4)	84 (8)	112 (7)	202 (12)	226 (14)	+140%	80%	+102%

Medicare and Other Entitlements	71 (14)	225 (20)	246 (16)	326 (20)	379 (23)	45%	33%	54%
Net Interest	33 (6)	98 (9)	220 (15)	247 (15)	212 (13)	152%	12%	-4%
Receipts and Deposit Insurance	-27 (-5)	-38 (-3)	23 (2)	-47 (-3)	-60 (-3)	n.a.	n.a.	n.a.

Sources: Executive Office of the President, *Budget of the United States Government, Fiscal Year 1998: Historical Tables* (February 1997), p. 109; Office of the Under Secretary of Defense, Comptroller, *National Defense Budget Estimates for Fiscal Year 1997* (Department of Defense, 1996), p. 39 (for deflators).

Notes: Numbers in parentheses show spending as a percentage of the federal total for that year. "n.a." means not applicable.

The average from 1962–1995 for international affairs spending was $20 billion and that for national defense was $310 billion. Relative to those averages, the 2002 projections for international affairs and defense would be down 15 percent and 20 percent, respectively. The president's projections for 2002 are based on Office of Management and Budget economic assumptions; they would have to be lower, on average, under Congressional Budget Office assumptions.

Percentages may not add up exactly to 100 because of rounding. Categories shown are those used in the Budget Enforcement Act, except that receipts and deposit insurance are combined into one category for this chart.

One consequence of recent budget cuts, the closing of several U.S. embassies and consulates to save State Department dollars, is a false economy at best and may create an image of American withdrawal from the world at worst. Brazil, Mexico, Indonesia, Thailand, the Philippines, Egypt, Turkey, France, Italy, and Germany are among the important countries where consulates have been closed. And our ability to open new facilities is limited. For example, we negotiated for the right to have five consulates in China but for budgetary reasons have only opened four. To compound the handicap, the State Department has had to scale back travel allowances for U.S. diplomatic personnel in that country, who now must cover greater distances than expected because of the reduced number of consulates. State Department budget levels are not drastically inadequate, but they are too low—and it would be imprudent to let the problem get much worse before redressing it.

The United States is being forced to choose, sometimes arbitrarily, which situations to address and which to ignore. This is a particular problem in countries at risk for political upheaval and violence. In the last two years, the United States did not have enough money to aid conflict resolution efforts in Liberia, Burundi, Rwanda, and Angola. Instead, it had to choose among them. Institutional development, such as improvement of police forces, courts, and prisons, suffered—with consequences for political stability already observable in Central Africa in recent months. Next time, we may not be so fortunate as to have a local army alleviate a major humanitarian crisis as effectively as the Zairian Tutsi appear to have done in the fall of 1996. At that point, our choice may be between ignoring our values and the plight of fellow human beings or using our own military forces to patch up a problem that should have been prevented.

Other examples, generally of less compelling immediate significance but still of concern, now abound. Some aid promised Turkey had to be rerouted at the last minute to support reforms in Haiti and funds designated for Russia had to be raided to help Mongolia. Money promised El Salvador and Guatemala to help demobilize opposing armies as required under peace accords was delivered much more slowly than intended. Support that the United States had hoped to provide nongovernmental organizations in Cuba and China that promote human rights and democracy was not available in the end. Given the U.S. concern about those two countries, ignoring whatever opportunities there may be to broaden and strengthen independent political actors within them seems unwise.

The United States has also fallen short on its commitments to help fund institutions such as the World Bank, International Development Association, and U.N. system. This practice is generally an unpromising way to attempt to win an argument about policy reforms in those bodies.

Other foreign assistance resources, already in gradual decline for a number of years, are now shrinking rapidly as well. This is happening at just the moment when the end of superpower ideological competition and a strong global consensus in favor of the marketplace present opportunities to help a number of countries become full-fledged members of the international economic and political system. In other words, not only are we increasing the risks of global violence, terrorism, overpopulation, and environmental catastrophe, we are forsaking opportunities to improve the United States' own economic well-being and reinforce its reputation as a beacon of economic and political rights for all.

Being involved in countries with diplomatic presence and foreign aid works in favor of U.S. interests. In Latin America, for example, goods from the United States comprise 57 percent of all imports regionwide—but 71 percent of the total in those six countries where we have given most of our aid. In Indonesia, a few million dollars in assistance to privatize energy production opened the door for a U.S. firm to win a $2 billion contract. An absolute majority of the dollar-value growth in U.S. exports is now to developing countries. (And in the short term, much foreign aid spending winds up back in the hands of U.S. firms.)[2]

In the specific area of agricultural development, it turns out—paradoxically, perhaps—that the more countries improve their own food production, the more food they import from the United

---

[2] Barry M. Blechman, *Foreign Assistance: What's in It for Americans?* (Washington, D.C.: Business Alliance for International Economic Development, 1996).

States. As countries' agricultural outputs increase, their wealth typically does too, providing the means and the desire for foodstuffs such as wheat and coarse grains that the United States specializes in producing.[3]

DEEPER CUTS WOULD BE UNACCEPTABLE

AS PROBLEMATIC as the spending cuts to date have been, much worse things may be in store. Unlike the case of the Pentagon budget, the international affairs account has not enjoyed even partial protection during the 1995 and 1996 deficit-elimination processes.

In early 1997, the president released his 1998 budget request that anticipated a further decline in real funding for international affairs from $19.6 billion to $16.8 billion by 2002 (see figure 2). That is the relatively good news. The bad news is that under the congressional budget-balancing resolution of April 1996, international spending would drop to $13 billion, or 30 percent less than its current level and 45 percent below its 1980–95 average. (All of these figures are expressed in terms of constant 1997 dollars.) That would be less than at any time since 1955, as figure 3 shows. The president's own 1996 plan would reduce funds to virtually the same levels, if it is modified to use the Congressional Budget Office's economic assumptions of early 1996 and defense is spared from any cuts beyond those already planned.

The improved deficit picture of early 1997 suggests that cuts would not be quite this severe under a revised budget-balancing plan. But even a reduction in real international discretionary spending to $15 billion could do grievous damage.

Consider the implications of such a spending level. One way to reach it would be to take $2 billion more out of development aid for poorer countries, $1 billion out of annual aid to the Middle East, $0.5 billion out of government support for U.S. business as well as U.N. costs, and a final $0.5 billion out of the State Department.

---

[3] Congressional Budget Office, Agricultural Progress in the Third World and Its Effect on U.S. Farm Exports (May 1989), pp. ix–xxvii.

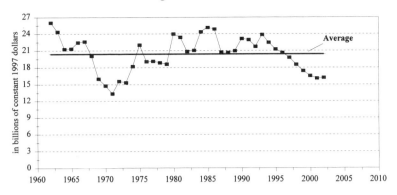

Figure 2. U.S. International Spending, 1962–2002

Source: Executive Office of the President, *Historical Tables: Budget of the United States Government for Fiscal Year 1997,* 1996, p. 109.

Notes: Data until 1996 are historical; figures from that point on are projections for the president's request for fiscal year 1997. They are based on OMB's relatively optimistic economic assumptions of early 1996; a more pessimistic forecast would imply a need for deeper cuts somewhere in the federal budget, possibly including international programs, in order to eliminate the deficit. Figures are outlays and use the definition of international discretionary spending from the Budget Enforcement Act, which includes funding for the State Department, U.N. peacekeeping, and other activities as well as foreign aid. The president's 1998 budget request changes the curve only slightly; it would terminate at the slightly higher level of $16.8 billion if based on the more recent budget.

The cut in development aid might, for example, be met by ending virtually all U.S. bilateral and multilateral support for development in Africa—leaving the European countries with primary responsibility for helping that troubled continent. (Outside of the Middle East, no other major region gets enough U.S. development aid to absorb a funding cut of that magnitude by itself; an alternative to cutting aid to Africa might be ending all U.S. contributions to both Latin American and South Asian countries.) The reduction in assistance to the Middle East might significantly affect Jordan and the West Bank and Gaza, possibly increasing the risks of economic discontent and political unrest within their populations and harming the peace process.

The decline in State's budget, a 20 percent real funding reduction, could be realized through a number of approaches—none of them appealing. For example, we could eliminate 100 of our smallest

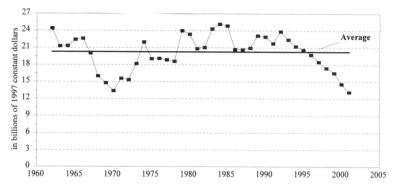

Figure 3. International Spending, 1962–2002
(projections based on Congress's 1996 budget plan)
Source: Executive Office of the President, *Historical Tables: Budget of the United States Government for Fiscal Year 1997,* 1996, p. 109.
Notes: Data until 1996 are historical; figures from that point on are projections. Figures are outlays and use the definition of international discretionary spending from the Budget Enforcement Act, which includes funding for the State Department, U.N. peacekeeping, military aid, international broadcasting, and other activities as well as development aid.

embassies and consulates, or close 50 of the smallest ones while making staff cuts of about 15 percent at the remainder. Depending on the approach, a number of the following consequences could be expected:

- Our monitoring of respect for intellectual property rights in Brazil, Indonesia, and China could suffer.
- Our efforts to help Mexico crack down on the drug trade and monitor its progress in doing so could be degraded.
- Our ability to understand major political factions and leaders in the Middle East could be compromised.
- Extremist Sudanese sheiks might more easily slip past our eyes and gain access to U.S. territory.
- The diplomatic reporting commonly done by our embassies could end in a country that is on the precipice of civil violence, impeding our ability to use suasion and negotiation to head off a major humanitarian emergency.

Those who advocate sharp reductions in international spending generally fail to recognize the potential ramifications of their positions, such as those just cited. They may be prepared to see one account or another savaged but would probably find at least one of the above-mentioned consequences of drastic cuts extremely unpalatable. Yet it would be difficult to avoid such cuts in Mideast and development aid, as well as funding for diplomacy and export promotion, regardless of the persuasiveness of their advocates within the U.S. political process. Those areas are where the money is—and if international spending cuts cumulatively approaching 50 percent in magnitude are made, it will be very hard if not impossible to spare them.

Cutting resources for foreign affairs does not make any sense for the world in which we live. Instead, U.S. international spending should increase from its 1997 level of $19.6 billion. Due to fiscal realities, increases should be as modest and targeted as possible. But to protect and promote U.S. interests abroad, a total international discretionary spending level of at least $21 billion is needed in 1998 (see table 2). That amount should be adjusted in the years ahead to keep up with inflation.

As a practical matter, that outlay level would require discretionary budget authority of around $22 billion in 1998. (Budget authority is akin to new money in the bank against which to enter into contractual agreements or write checks; outlays or spending are akin to the payments that result when those checks are cashed.) But restoring dependable and adequate resource levels for the foreseeable future matters more than hitting a specific number in 1998.

The above numbers each would need to be about $1 billion greater were it not for specific reforms that can and should be made in U.S. international activities. Specifically, cuts in the PL 480 Title I program, U.S. dues to the U.N. system, and certain administrative functions within the various U.S. foreign affairs agencies can save a total of $500 million a year. Another $500 million can be saved by reducing development aid to countries with unpromising economic policies—although that amount, rather than being redirected to other programs, should be kept within the development accounts and used to restore adequate funding to countries with good

Table 2. Recommended Outlays for U.S. International Affairs
($billion)

Objective or Activity	Annual Funding Level
1997 International Discretionary Spending	19.6
Added Costs	
Additional Flexible Money in Economic Support Fund	0.6
Additional Funds for Computers etc. for State Department	0.15
Restructuring/Buyout Account for State Department (1998 and 1999)	0.1
Funds to Partially Restore Bilateral Aid to Earlier Levels	0.5
Arrearages at United Nations, including Peacekeeping	0.2
Arrearages at International Development Association (IDA), Other Multilateral Organizations[a]	0.2
Subtotal, Added Costs	1.75
Recommended Savings	
Bureaucratic Consolidation, Reorganization (State etc.)	0.15
Cuts in U.S. Secretariat, Multilateral Development Agencies	0.1
Termination of PL 480 Titles I and III	0.25
Subtotal, Savings	0.5
Grand Total	
1998 International Discretionary Spending (including inflation adjustment)	21.0

[a] Budget authority should also increase relative to its 1997 level by $700 million to satisfy future requirements.

policies (in many cases, their aid has been cut severely in the last few years).

While higher than today's spending or the amounts proposed by the president and Congress, a $21 billion outlay level would remain below the 1980–95 average of roughly $23 billion (again, in 1997 dollars). Moreover, the international affairs budget would still be doing more than its fair share to balance the budget by 2002. Under this proposal, it would be cut more in percentage terms than domestic discretionary spending or any major entitlement program over the 1990–2002 period.

The balance of this report considers in more detail the specific objectives of U.S. foreign policy and the challenges of pursuing each in the current international environment. It also considers the potential for various types of budgetary savings. It concludes by laying out a political strategy for restoring broad domestic support for international affairs, a strategy that must begin with the president but involve the full participation of Congress as well.

THE INTERNATIONAL DISCRETIONARY BUDGET

THERE IS a plethora of ways to look at the international budget that can confound all but the most meticulous and knowledgeable bureaucrats. Both opponents and proponents often further confuse the debate by taking numbers out of context. For example, those advocates of foreign assistance and diplomacy who imply that funding has already been cut 50 percent relative to the norms of an earlier era overstate their case.[4] Unfortunately, they may wind up being right if we do not change course.

This report focuses on actual government spending or outlays, rather than year-to-year budget authority. Budget authority fluctuates too much from one year to the next for reasons that have more to do with financial aberrations than policy.

---

[4] To be specific, they often use as their point of comparison a year in which budget authority was much higher than in any year before or after due to emergency relief for drought in Africa, temporary increases in assistance to the Middle East, and other unusual and coinciding events.

Table 3. The U.S. International Discretionary Account
(1997 $billion)

Type of Spending	Estimated 1997 Outlays	Running Total
Development AID		
Multilateral Aid		
Development Banks	1.7	1.7
Voluntary Contributions to UNICEF, etc.	0.3	2.0
Bilateral Aid		
Development Assistance	2.3	4.3
Economic Support Funds	2.4	6.7
PL 480 Food Aid	1.1	7.8
Refugee Assistance	0.9	8.7
Peace Corps, Other	0.5	9.2
Other Foreign Assistance		
Aid to Central/Eastern Europe, Former Soviet Union	1.2	10.4
Foreign Military Financing	3.3	13.7
International Military Education and Training	0.05	13.8
Narcotics Control	0.2	14.0
IAEA, Korean Reactor Deal	0.11	14.1
U.S. Information Agency	1.2	15.3
U.N. Peacekeeping	0.35	15.6

Breakdowns of expected spending in 1997 are shown in table 3. To highlight a couple of key points, most of the international account is foreign aid—for development in poorer countries, political and economic reform in the former Communist states, or security assistance to Israel and Egypt. The vast preponderance is given bilaterally; table 4 shows the major recipients of U.S. bilateral aid in 1996 (not counting Nunn-Lugar aid for the former Soviet republics, which comes out of the defense budget).

Table 3, continued

Type of Spending	Estimated 1997 Outlays	Running Total
Bilateral and Multilateral Diplomacy		
State Department	2.5	18.1
ACDA, Other	0.2	18.3
U.S. Secretariat, Other U.S. Organizations (administrative costs)	0.9	19.2
Business		
Export-Import Bank, Other	0.4	19.6
Addendum: Aid Funded Out of the U.S. Military Budget		
Nunn-Lugar Cooperative Threat Reduction Aid for former U.S.S.R.	0.4	
U.S. Military Costs in Indirect Support of U.N. Peace Operations	1.5 to 3.5	

Source: Executive Office of the President, *Budget of the United States Government, Fiscal Year 1998* (February 1997), pp. 252-3.
Notes: Function 150 includes roughly $5 billion in negative spending (receipts from foreign governments and the like), so it totals about $15 billion in outlays in 1997.

It is not yet possible to estimate the (mostly unreimbursed) U.S. military costs in support of U.N. peace operations in 1997. The estimate here reflects the 1994–96 annual average.

In quantitative terms, $4 billion out of the $19.6 billion in international discretionary spending is for diplomacy, U.N. dues, and support for U.S. business overseas. A bit more than $6 billion is for foreign aid focused on specific U.S. national interests like security aid to the Middle East, transition assistance for the former Soviet republics, and public diplomacy through the Voice of America. About $9 billion is to help developing countries.

While examining these numbers, it is appropriate to ask how they

Table 4. Major Recipients of U.S. Bilateral Aid, 1996
($million of obligations)

Recipient	Amount	Recipient	Amount
1. Israel	3,000	9. South Africa	125
2. Egypt	2,270	10. Ethiopia	115
3. Russia	320	11. Rwanda	110
4. Bosnia	310	12. Peru	95
5. Ukraine	245	13. Armenia	95
6. Jordan	180	14. Bolivia	85
7. India	160	15. West Bank/Gaza	75
8. Haiti	125	16. Bangladesh	75

Source: U.S. Agency for International Development, *Congressional Presentation Summary Tables, Fiscal Year 1997* (July 1996), pp. 38-41.

compare to corresponding numbers from other industrialized countries whose global interests are similar to our own. Consider, for example, our development aid to poorer countries, comprising about half of total U.S. international spending.

Much is often made of the fact that after implementing the Marshall Plan and then dominating development assistance through the 1960s, the United States has now greatly slipped in its position as a lead donor. For the most recent year for which comparative data is available, 1995, the United States was essentially tied in absolute dollar terms with Germany and France for second place on the major donors list. Each of the three provided roughly $8 billion in official development assistance (ODA), well behind Japan with its aid levels of $12 billion to $14 billion a year (depending on exactly how one measures, as shown in table 5). U.S. ODA now represents only about one-sixth of the global total and could drop to just one-tenth under the proposed budget-balancing schemes.

This U.S. ODA budget translates into a very small percentage of the country's GDP. Among all Organization for Economic Cooperation and Development (OECD) countries, the United States is the least generous by this metric. The United States now gives about 0.10 percent of its GDP in official development assis-

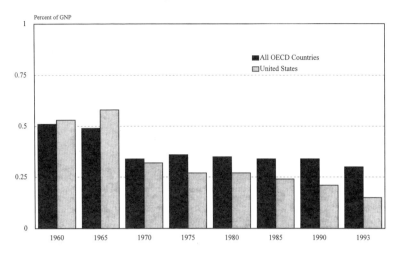

Figure 4. Economic Burden of Foreign Aid, 1960–93

Sources: World Bank, *World Development Report 1980* (New York: Oxford
University Press, 1980), pp. 140–41; World Bank, *World Development Report 1995*
(New York: Oxford University Press, 1995), p. 196.
Notes: Under the president's budget request for fiscal year 1997—relatively favorable
to international programs compared with Congress's latest detailed plan—aid would
drop by 30 percent in real terms by 2002, relative to its 1993 level. Thus, it would
decline to 0.08 percent of GNP (that is, assuming that ODA would be cut by the
same fraction as would overall international spending). From 1960 to 1993, U.S.
overseas assistance dropped from representing 58 percent of the world total to 18
percent.

tance; by comparison, the OECD average is nearly 0.30 percent (see
figure 4).

It is hardly troublesome that the United States gives far less than
called for by the U.N. General Assembly. The United Nations' official target is that donors provide 0.70 of their GDP in aid, but the
case for giving this much money is weak on developmental grounds.[5]
Nor is it necessarily inappropriate that the United States devotes a

___

[5] A forthcoming study that attempts to calculate an optimal amount of global ODA from
the "bottom up" argues that donors should increase their average aid from just under 0.30
percent of GDP to 0.35 percent. See Michael O'Hanlon and Carol Graham, *A Half Penny
on the Federal Dollar: The Future of Development Aid* (Washington, D.C.: Brookings,
1997).

Table 5. Foreign Aid Donations by OECD Countries, 1995

Donor Country	Net Official ODA, 1995 (current $billion)	Net Official ODA (constant 1997 $billion)	ODA as Percent of GNP	Estimated Grant-Equivalent Value of ODA (constant 1997 $billion)
Japan	14.5	15.1	.28	12.0
France	8.4	8.8	.55	7.5
Germany	7.5	7.8	.31	7.0
United States	7.3	7.6	.10	7.5
Netherlands	3.3	3.4	.80	3.0
United Kingdom	3.2	3.3	.29	3.0
Canada	2.1	2.2	.39	2.0
Sweden	2.0	2.1	.89	2.0
Denmark	1.6	1.7	.97	—

Italy	1.5	1.6	.14	1.5
Spain	1.3	1.4	.23	1.0
Norway	1.24	1.3	.87	1.0
Australia	1.14	1.2	.34	1.0
Switzerland	1.08	1.13	.34	1.0
Belgium	1.03	1.07	.38	1.0
Austria	.75	0.8	.32	0.5
Finland	.39	0.4	.32	0.5
Portugal	.27	.28	.27	—
Ireland	.14	.15	.27	.15
New Zealand	.12	.13	.23	.10
Luxembourg	.07	.07	.38	.05

Source: Organization for Economic Cooperation and Development, *Development Cooperation, 1995* (Paris: OECD, 1996), pp. A4 and A47; and Organization for Economic Cooperation and Development, "Financial Flows to Developing Countries in 1995: Sharp Decline in Official Aid; Private Flows Rise," Press Release (OECD, 1996).

Notes: Since some aid is given as loans at concessional rates, its grant-equivalent component is less than the nominal size of the loan. Thus, a country's actual aid is generally somewhat smaller than its ODA. Here, the estimates of grant aid are approximate. They apply the grant-like aid ratios of 1993–94 to 1995 ODA.

smaller share of its GDP to official aid than do other donors. Unlike most other donors, this country provides a sum representing another 0.10 percent of its GDP in non-ODA assistance (as shown in table 6), making for a more respectable (if still low) total aid level equivalent to about 0.2 percent of its GDP.

Also, comparisons based solely on ODA ignore the fact that the U.S. military makes unrivaled contributions to global political stability. That stability permits international commerce to flourish, benefiting rich and poorer countries alike (see table 6). Looked at in this way, the United States devotes about 4.0 percent of its GDP to foreign policy activities advancing common Western and international interests, while Japan devotes about 1.3 percent to such purposes, NATO Europe 2.7 percent in aggregate, and several other Western states an average of 2.4 percent. The United States also has fewer barriers to imports than do most other donors, providing a type of self-help opportunity that is more important than aid for middle-income developing countries.

But these arguments notwithstanding, the fact that U.S. aid continues to deteriorate is of serious concern. For one thing, as a consequence of these cuts the United States may lose influence in the international financial institutions. Its generous development assistance of earlier decades, technical expertise in realms such as agricultural research and family planning, huge economy, and superpower status have enabled it to shape the multilateral agenda in ways consistent with U.S. interests. The president of the World Bank is always an American. The World Bank and International Monetary Fund are based in Washington, where they can be lobbied to support U.S. interests on issues such as aid to Russia and the Mexico bailout. And the United States' substantial leverage in these institutions has helped us catalyze special efforts such as the West Bank/Gaza and Bosnia development and reconstruction plans. But the United States will not continue to enjoy all these prerogatives if its aid budget keeps dropping. Other donors are telling us as much.

The following discussion, organized conceptually to highlight the different purposes of U.S. international spending, identifies the potential for savings but also the need for more adequate resources if U.S.

Table 6. Overall Foreign Policy Spending as Percent of GDP (1995)

	NATO Europe (excluding Greece and Turkey)	Canada, Australia, New Zealand, Sweden, Switzerland, and Austria	Japan	United States
Official Development Assistance	0.37	0.34	0.28	0.1
Other Aid-Related Activities including Peacekeeping (approximate)	0.075	0.025	0.01	0.1
Defense Spending	2.3	2.0	1.0	3.9
Total	2.7	2.4	1.3	4.1

Sources: Organization for Economic Cooperation and Development, "Financial Flows to Developing Countries in 1995," June 11, 1996; Stockholm International Peace Research Institute, *SIPRI Yearbook* (Oxford: Oxford University Press, 1996), pp. 365–70; International Institute for Strategic Studies, *The Military Balance 1995–1996* (New York: Oxford University Press, 1995), p. 39; World Bank, *World Development Report 1995* (New York: Oxford University Press, 1995), p. 196.

foreign policy activities are to help build a peaceful and prosperous 21st century.[6]

PROMOTING PEACE

IMMEDIATELY RELEVANT to our global leadership position are flexible funds to support specific initiatives related to politics and conflict resolution. Economic support funds (ESF), unencumbered by procedural obstacles or earmarking, are usually the best tool for such purposes, although accounts such as foreign military financing and international military education and training (IMET) can also be useful. It would be sensible to increase funding for these accounts —the bulk of which now is devoted to Egypt and Israel—by about $600 million a year to be able to help other countries when circumstances require it.[7]

That amount would be ample for responding to about two unexpected major crises a year, roughly the pace at which they are arising. It would also be sufficient for several other initiatives focused on building governmental and/or nongovernmental institutions in countries from Cuba to Rwanda to China to Haiti.

To be more specific, flexible bilateral funds can help the Rwandan legal system get on its feet and try war criminals, induce Kurdish factions in Iraq to cooperate with each other and pay monitors of a cease-fire between them, give the Haitian government incen-

---

[6] This discussion uses categories similar to those of the Clinton administration's proposed rewriting of the Foreign Assistance Act, a bill that was considered but turned down by Congress in 1994. The categories of "promoting sustainable development" and "providing humanitarian relief" are aggregated here, but have the same meaning as in the Clinton bill. As used here, the category of "advancing diplomacy" focuses only on U.S. diplomacy and that of "promoting peace" focuses only on foreign assistance. Parts of the Clinton administration's categories for advancing diplomacy and promoting peace are treated here under another heading, "core U.N. functions," that includes peacekeeping as well as the U.N. bureaucracy. The Task Force has no recommendations for major change for the last two Clinton categories, "building democracy" and "promoting prosperity."

[7] Alternatively, depending on need, some small fraction of that $600 million total might instead be provided through an expansion of the IMET program and the foreign military financing (FMF) program.

tive to reform its economic system by promising it immediate balance-of-payments support, and help convince the government of Burundi to broaden its ethnic representation by promising the same.[8]

Although the United States will often be acting in concert with other outside parties in such settings, it needs the flexibility and rapidity that bilateral aid can provide. That also can allow it to pursue objectives of particular interest to the United States even if other countries do not enthusiastically support them.

Use of flexible funds like ESF does not require detailed project proposals, lengthy contract bidding processes, or accomplishment of other time-consuming objectives. ESF funds are high-leverage instruments of diplomacy that were once much greater in size and should be somewhat larger today. They can make the difference between war and peace, chaos and stability, friendship and hostility.

ADVANCING U.S. DIPLOMACY

ALTHOUGH THE U.S. STATE DEPARTMENT is in need of further management reforms and streamlining, it also has a host of unmet needs. The most pressing is to modernize information technology in Washington and overseas. Doing so would better serve not only State but the dozens of other federal agencies co-located with it overseas.

The necessary amounts of money are not small—roughly $750 million—but can be spread over a five-year time frame. An additional $100 million a year for 1998 and 1999 would facilitate restructuring through such mechanisms as employee "buyouts" and early retirements. These amounts represent a scaled-back alternative to what the State Department itself believes it requires. But in light of the country's fiscal situation and the need to prioritize, it should suffice for truly pressing needs.

---

[8] On the acute need for money for such purposes, see for example, Jim Hoagland, "The Real Cash Scandal," *Washington Post,* October 24, 1996, p. A21.

The requirement for added money may be temporary. Consolidation within or between foreign policy agencies may eventually allow savings of a comparable magnitude that would permit State and affiliated agencies to make do with their 1997 level of resources. But the need for adequate funding cannot wait.

Rationale for a Larger Budget

The Department of State is sorely in need of substantial capital investments. Although budgets for facilities did go up considerably in the 1980s, the increments were devoted largely to establishing new embassies and improving security at existing sites, and they did not adequately address the realm of information technology. At present, about half of State Department personnel do not have direct access to modern computing and communications equipment. About $200 million a year over five years is needed to redress this situation. Some money can be found in existing budgets if State makes information technology a higher priority. But real funding increases of roughly $150 million a year, for a five-year total of $750 million, do appear necessary. These added funds could be placed in a special, protected account for capital investment and appropriated on a "no year" basis that allows flexibility in how they are spent.

In addition, the State Department is not optimally structured for the challenges of today's world, and some reorganization would be sensible. A modest fund from which to provide compensation for those affected by downsizing and consolidation would be desirable. Roughly $100 million a year for the first two years would be adequate for this purpose.

No other increases in State's budget appear necessary at this time—even though the department has calculated that it requires another $1.5 billion for improvements in plant and equipment, and even though its operating budget has become strained. Reforms and reengineering can be relied upon to take care of these other needs without additional real resources.

To see why, consider State's normal operating budget (see figure 5). Even after factoring out security costs and expenditures on overseas facilities, it remains 50 percent, or $600 million a year, greater than the $1.2 billion level in 1980 (as expressed in 1997 dollars). And

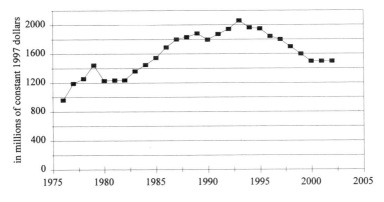

Figure 5. State Department Operating Costs
(not including security activities)
Source: U.S. Department of State.
Note: Projections are based on the president's budget request for fiscal year 1997 and assume proportionate cuts for all parts of budget function 153. Costs are shown in terms of outlays.

proceeds from processing visas and passports now provide it another $50 million a year with which to pay for operations.

Yet in order to meet budgetary constraints, a number of consulates as well as several small embassies have regrettably been closed. Shortened work hours are in effect at some posts, and other false economies have been imposed due to a shortage of operating money.

Why, given the increase in real funding levels, is this so? Largely because of increased costs and responsibilities. Roughly $50 million a year more is now needed due to a weakening of the U.S. dollar, which makes operating overseas more expensive (although the dollar gained appreciably in 1996, it is still significantly weaker than 15 or 20 years ago). At least $100 million more is needed to operate about 20 new missions in the former Soviet republics and former Yugoslavia as well as Albania and Vietnam. A slightly lesser sum is needed for increased workloads processing passports and visas. (State also spends substantially more money than formerly supporting the overseas efforts of other U.S. agencies. But under management reforms now being put in place, it is expected to soon recoup that amount—about $100 million a year—in fuller reimbursement for the services it provides.)[9]

Above and beyond these specific added costs, today's State Department is expected to do more than it had to do in 1980. U.S. trade and investment overseas have increased greatly. In addition to helping U.S. businesses, Americans traveling abroad, and a constantly expanding flow of visitors to the United States, diplomats now are spending more time on the problems of terrorism, proliferation, and international crime. The 1980 real dollar level is thus an imperfect benchmark for today's needs, even after the above adjustments are made.

Still, at this point State does not need more operating money so much as a change in the way it does business. In keeping with Vice President Al Gore's 1995 directives, State and other foreign affairs agencies should move to reduce duplication among policy and program elements. For example, the reviews of redundancies in humanitarian, environmental, and other functional areas that the vice president ordered should be resurrected and pursued.[10]

Reforms and Savings

Questions about consolidation of U.S. foreign affairs agencies are important and worthy of thoughtful debate. They are also within the purview of both the president and Congress. They should be addressed by the White House and Capitol Hill together—particularly since the odds of obtaining adequate funding will be greatly improved by reaching agreement on how best to structure the executive branch for post–Cold War foreign policymaking.

One means of addressing the problem of agency reform and consolidation could be the creation of a commission to study the matter and make recommendations. The commission would be appointed by the president and Congress and report to both. It would examine not only the Agency for International Development

---

[9] See Congressional Budget Office, *Reducing the Deficit: Spending and Revenue Options* (August 1996), pp. 193-4; General Accounting Office, *State Department: Options for Addressing Possible Budget Reductions,* GAO/NSIAD-96-124 (August 1996), pp. 1-9.

[10] See Press Release, Office of the Vice President, January 25, 1995.

(AID), the Arms Control and Disarmament Agency (ACDA), the U.S. Information Agency (USIA), and State but other agencies relevant to U.S. foreign policy and matters of congressional jurisdiction and organization as well.

A cautionary note for this future task force: potential savings figures appear to have been bandied about rather inexactly in the consolidation debate so far and to have been exaggerated. Experience in the mergers and acquisitions world and elsewhere suggests that when two corporations with similar businesses merge, aggregate administrative costs typically decline by roughly 10 percent (although there is admittedly wide variance from case to case). Much of State, with an operating budget of $2 billion a year, does business unrelated to that of ACDA, AID, and USIA. These latter three agencies have combined operating expenses of nearly $1 billion a year. Since their functions only partially overlap with State's, it would be unrealistic to expect savings of 10 percent of their aggregate budgets. Rather than anticipate annual savings of $300 million, therefore, something in the range of $100 million to $200 million seems more realistic—although still undoubtedly difficult to achieve.

A number of alternative structural models exist between wholesale consolidation and the status quo. Whichever might ultimately be recommended and adopted, steps can be taken now to consolidate administrative support activities common to the foreign affairs agencies. The elimination of duplicative foreign affairs administrative functions was mandated by the vice president in 1995 and would be a logical follow-on to the recent creation of the international cooperative administrative support system (ICASS) overseas. In any event, and certainly as a precursor to administrative merger, State should reengineer all of its support elements as it is now doing with its worldwide logistics system. This move would permit the reallocation of some of the excessively large Washington overhead budgets to field operations.

Additional savings, although not necessarily to be found within the international account, might also be achieved by restructuring embassies and consulates abroad. The approach would consist of giving each chief of mission the authority to restructure his or her mission by increasing certain types of officers and experts from var-

ious agencies while decreasing others) generally with the added pro-
viso that net costs would have to go down. The downsides to this
option are its complexity and the unlikelihood that Congress will
endorse the idea of giving State Department employees power to
reduce other agencies' personnel and budgets.

The changes that will be brought about if the Office of Management and Budget (OMB) ensures the strict implementation of
ICASS may also have the effect of reducing overall U.S. government expenditures overseas. When each agency is compelled to pay
its full share of overseas costs and to justify those costs to its respec-
tive appropriations subcommittees, overseas staffing may well
become leaner and expenditures more frugal.

PROMOTING SUSTAINABLE DEVELOPMENT
AND PROVIDING RELIEF

TRYING TO HELP poorer countries improve their economies and the
well-being of their people is a vast enterprise, concerning more than
half the world's population and consuming almost half the dollars
the United States spends on international affairs. The Task Force
recommends a number of savings in this area but a net increase of
roughly $1 billion in annual funding (not counting the recom-
mended increases in ESF funds). In effect, that increase would simply make up for about half of the ground lost since the early 1990s.

Requirements for Added Funding
In the last few years, two separate but related crises have developed
in U.S. funding for overseas development. First, overall resource
levels have dwindled; annual U.S. overseas development aid (ODA)
has declined from a Cold War average of around $12 billion to about
$9 billion in 1997. (Much of U.S. ODA is found in budget func-
tion 151, although 151 now also funds non-ODA aid to the former
Communist states. The history of 151 spending is displayed in figure 6.) Since most U.S. aid is disbursed through bilateral programs,
the largest effects of these cuts have been felt at AID and other U.S.
organizations. Second, specific U.S. financial obligations to mul-

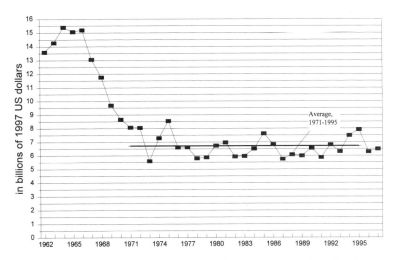

Figure 6. U.S. Development and Humanitarian Aid, Budget
Function 151 Outlays, 1962–97

Sources: Executive Office of the President, *Historical Tables: Budget of the
United States Government for Fiscal Year 1998* (February 1997), pp. 50–54; Larry
Nowels, "Foreign Operations for Appropriations for FY 1997: Funding and Policy
Issues." 96–455 F.

Notes: GDP deflators were used to put data into 1997 dollars. This table includes
development aid for the former Soviet republics as well as Central and Eastern
Europe, meaning that $1.2 billion in current spending does not go to developing
countries in the commonly understood sense of the word. Outlays for 151 will decline
to $5.5 billion in 2002, even as spending on former Communist states remains $850
million.

tilateral institutions that this country did much to establish have been
shortchanged.

Development aid is important for a number of reasons. First,
if used properly to support economic growth in countries with
sound policies, it can advance U.S. commercial interests. As noted
earlier, most of the growth in U.S. exports is now to developing countries, and most future growth will probably occur there as well. Second, it can serve Americans' humanitarian interests, particularly as
regards the world's poorest and youngest inhabitants and those most
afflicted by conflict, natural disaster, or disease and hunger. Third,
it can offer hope and economic opportunity to individuals who oth-

erwise might be attracted by extremist ideologies and organizations—the consequences of which can be viewed in places such as the Middle East and Bosnia. Fourth, it can improve the odds for long-term global environmental sustainability by protecting soils, aquifers, forests, and oceans and helping to keep global population growth on a reasonable course.

Even without a full review of the effectiveness of development aid today, it appears safe to conclude that certain types of aid are at present insufficient. Table 7 shows evidence of the good that many development programs have been able to help effect throughout the world; more could be accomplished with adequate resources.[11] And lest anyone be misled by the recent increases in private capital flowing to developing countries, the poorest of them still depend heavily on foreign assistance (see figure 7). A prudent regard for their citizens' welfare would lead the United States to provide at least an additional half billion dollars a year for these activities through bilateral means.[12]

Another requirement for more adequate development funding is to pay fully U.S. shares of capital replenishments at the international financial institutions. Most notable in this group is the International Development Association (IDA), which provides support for the poorest of the world's countries. The United States has in the recent past provided about 15 percent of its development aid through multilateral organizations, only about half as much as most donors; now, the United States is letting that figure drop further.

Largely as a consequence of our arrearages, during the Clinton administration U.S. funding for poverty alleviation has declined more severely than other major types of foreign aid. An increase in bud-

---

[11] See, for example, David Gordon, Catherine Gwin, and Steven Sinding, "What Future for Aid?" Overseas Development Council and Henry Stimson Center, Washington, D.C., 1996.

[12] See James P. Grant, *The State of the World's Children 1994* (New York: Oxford University Press, 1993); World Bank, *World Development Report 1990*, *World Development Report 1991*, and *World Development Report 1992* (New York: Oxford University Press, 1990, 1991, and 1992), pp. 75-87, 55-8, and 172-4, respectively; Congressional Budget Office, *Enhancing U.S. Security Through Foreign Aid* (April 1994), pp. 49-64.

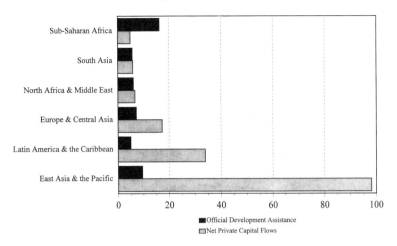

Figure 7. Recent Capital Flows to Developing Countries,
from all Sources ($billion)

Sources: Organization for Economic Cooperation and Development, *Development Cooperation 1995* (Paris: OECD, 1996), pp. A67, A96; World Bank, *World Debt Tables,* vol. 1 (Washington, D.C.: World Bank, 1996), p.11.
Note: Aid figures are annual averages for the two-year period 1993–94, the most recent for which data are available; private flows are for 1995.

get authority of about $700 million a year relative to the 1997 level would do much to solve this problem. It would allow the United States to restore funding for the international financial institutions to a level near the previous amount (requiring $500 million more than in 1997) and also add $200 million annually to make good on arrears over five years.[13] (In 1997, outlays are not as insufficient as budget authority. But outlays will soon decline severely as well, unless remedial action is taken.)

Keeping IDA in good financial condition makes sense on burden-sharing grounds; for every $1 that the United States contributes to it, other donors provide about $4. Also, the IDA, although part of the broader U.N. system, is not within its core elements but is affiliated with the American-led World Bank and is based in Washington. Its administration requires scrutiny but

---

[13] An argument could also be made for paying the arrearages more quickly, with corresponding increases in the budget for 1998 and slightly lower budgets down the road.

Table 7. Trends in Human Development by Region

	Sub-Saharan Africa	Arab States	South Asia	East Asia	Southeast Asia	Latin America, Caribbean
Life Expectancy (years)						
1960	40.0	46.7	43.8	47.5	45.3	56.0
1992	51.1	64.3	58.5	70.5	62.9	67.7
Infant Mortality (per thousand; deaths before first birthday)						
1960	165	165	164	146	126	105
1992	101	54	94	27	55	47
Access to Safe Water (%)						
1975–80	25	71	—	—	15	60
1988–91	45	79	—	—	53	79

Malnourished Children ((% under five)

1975	31	25	69	26	46	17
1990	31	20	59	21	34	10

Adult literacy (%)

1970	28	30	33	—	67	76
1992	51	57	47	—	86	86

Real GDP per Capita (in 1991 dollars; PPP measure)

1960	—	1,310	700	730	1,000	2,140
1991	—	4,420	1,260	3,210	3,420	5,360

Source: United Nations Development Program, *Human Development Report 1994* (New York: Oxford University Press, 1994), p. 207.
Note: PPP refers to the purchasing power parity measure, which gives a better indication of actual purchasing power for goods produced and consumed locally than does GDP calculated strictly according to the official exchange rate. Countries in the "East Asia" category are China, Hong Kong, North Korea, South Korea, and Mongolia; countries in "South Asia" are Afghanistan, Bangladesh, Bhutan, India, Iran, Maldives, Nepal, Pakistan, and Sri Lanka.

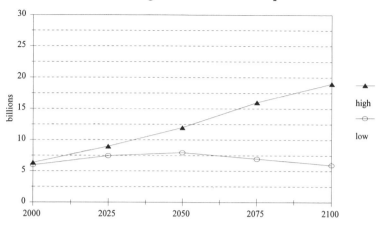

Figure 8. World Population Projections, 2000–2100
(high and low estimates)

Source: United Nations, *Long-Range World Population Projections* (New York: 1994), p.4.

Note: Among other demographic assumptions, the estimates presume that lifetime fertility rates per woman will eventually be 2.6 children (high estimate) or 1.6 children (low estimate) in countries that now have high population growth.

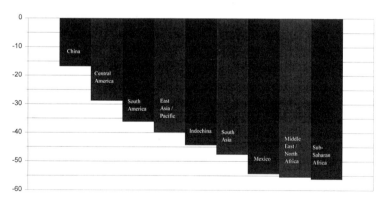

Figure 9. Change in Agricultural Land per Capita
(cumulative percentage change, 1961–1991

Source: Congressional Budget Office, "Assessing Threats to U.S. Security" (unpublished paper, May 1995), based on CD-ROM data from the World Bank.

Note: Total agricultural area is the total of unused arable land, permanent cropland, and permanent meadows and pastureland. Data for each country are weighted by the country's share of the region's population.

should cause fewer worries than certain institutions linked more close-ly to U.N. headquarters.

The stakes involved in these funding issues are potentially enor-mous. For example, today's world population of nearly six billion could double in the next century, placing huge strains on the envi-ronment. Or it could be limited—through family planning, improved child survival, and, in the longer term, more primary education for both girls and boys as well as policies advancing economic growth—to the much more modest increases suggested in figure 8. Even if global population does not grow much, however, agricultural yields per acre will need to keep increasing, since available farmland is lim-ited and the oceans are already being fished near their maximum sus-tainable potential (see figure 9). Donor-supported agricultural research can make a major difference in that regard as well.

Savings

In this area too, economies should be possible. For example, Title I of the PL 480 food program should be eliminated, and Title III phased out once the Title I debts that it is intended to address are liquidated. Potential annual savings would be about $250 million.[14]

In contrast to Title II, Title I is not used for disaster relief but to dispose of U.S. agricultural surpluses and to provide some ready cash for recipient governments. Those governments receive the food, which they sell in their home markets to generate additional bud-getary resources (denominated in local currency).

Yet Title I funds less than one percent of U.S. food exports, so it is much less critical for U.S. farmers than in the past. Even more importantly, it can set back the development of recipient countries' agricultural sectors and economies by depressing food prices and there-by discouraging production. In the end, Title I can work against U.S. farmers because countries mired in poverty do not buy near-ly as much U.S. food as the middle-income developing countries.

Savings could also come from rethinking which countries should receive aid. Although virtually any country should be provided human-

---

[14] See also Congressional Budget Office, *Reducing the Deficit: Spending and Revenue Options* (August 1996), pp. 193–202.

itarian relief in a dire moment of need, only those with good economic policies have a realistic chance of using economic aid to start on the path of sustainable growth. And only about half of the countries in the developing world now have such promising policies—realistic currency exchange rates, low trade barriers, low inflation, small budget deficits, minimal consumer and producer subsidies, and well-functioning legal systems.

During the Cold War, the United States sometimes continued to provide help to countries with poor economic policy fundamentals because of strategic considerations. At this point, however, aid can and should be much more selective.[15] The bilateral funds at issue may total $500 million or more and are found mostly in the development assistance account. However, in light of the overall decline in U.S. assistance that has already occurred over the last few years, these funds should not be cut from the aid budget. Rather, they should be redirected to countries with sound economic frameworks that are able to make good use of increased aid. Many of them could benefit from more resources than they are now receiving.

SUPPORTING CORE UNITED NATIONS FUNCTIONS

THE U.N. SECRETARIAT remains inefficient and probably overfunded. But U.S. arrears to the United Nations should be eliminated, and most dues paid in full in the future.

The United States Should Pay Peacekeeping Dues On Time and in Full
Although justifications exist for pushing the United Nations to make reforms and rethink peace operations, the newly formed U.S. habit of withholding payments to it is in our view unwise behavior on the part of the world's only superpower.[16]

---

[15] See Michael O'Hanlon and Carol Graham, *A Half Penny on the Federal Dollar: The Future of Development Aid* (Washington, D.C.: Brookings, 1997).
[16] For a similar view, see Shijuro Ogata and Paul Volcker, *Financing an Effective United Nations* (New York: Ford Foundation, 1993).

Even if we pay only 20 to 25 percent of total U.N. costs—in contrast to current assessments of 25 percent for regular activities and about 30 percent for peacekeeping—and even if the Secretariat is scaled back, U.S. payments need to increase. Our arrearages for peacekeeping together with the regular U.N. budget total slightly over $1 billion, according to the U.S. government. That amount includes roughly $700 million for peacekeeping dues, assuming a 25 percent rate of contribution starting in fiscal year 1996. (Since the United Nations has not yet recognized this reduced U.S. payment rate, it considers our arrearages to be about $200 million higher.) The rest is made up of about $350 million in dues to the United Nations and affiliated agencies such as the Food and Agricultural Organization—not counting contributions to groups like the Palestine Liberation Organization that the United States refuses to support as a matter of principle (the United Nations' number for our arrearages to the Secretariat and affiliated organizations is $150 million higher). The $1 billion in U.S. government-recognized arrearages should be paid in full.[17]

Although vigorous debate about peacekeeping policy is appropriate within this country, the United States has no excuse not to pay dues—especially since it could have prevented every single U.N. mission with its Security Council veto. Meanwhile, Americans should remember not only the potential difficulties of U.N. operations but the great promise they now offer, in an era no longer constrained by the threat of a Soviet Security Council veto, for managing the world's conflict zones multilaterally.

To be sure, severe difficulties have been encountered with U.N. missions in Somalia and Bosnia—mostly because of the inherent complexities of those situations and poor decision making by the Security Council countries that set the policy framework for the operations. Everything must be done to minimize the odds of similar problems in the future. But U.N. successes have been more common. They include, among others, the cases of Nicaragua, El

---

[17] Or at least nearly in full: allowance might be made for some partial "credit" for the military support we supply many U.N. peacekeeping missions, as recently suggested by President Reagan's U.N. ambassador, Jeanne Kirkpatrick.

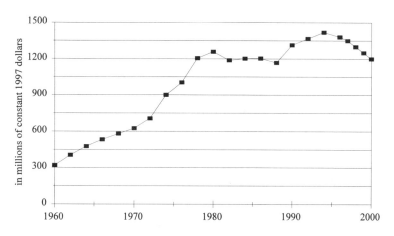

Figure 10. U.N. Regular Budget, 1960–2000
(projections based on U.N. budget plans)
Source: United Nations Information Center, "United Nations Regular Budget Appropriations," March 1996.
Note: These costs are for the U.N. Secretariat and for the basic administration of various U.N. specialized agencies. The amounts shown are for 12-month periods.

Salvador, Cambodia, the Golan Heights, Namibia, Eritrea, Mozambique, and Angola. U.N. efforts can often offer the United States a highly valuable choice between doing nothing and doing everything itself.[18]

It is impossible to calculate the resources that will be needed for peacekeeping in the future. But in rough terms, our overall annual contributions to the United Nations will probably have to increase by $200 million relative to the 1997 level for perhaps five years in order to pay arrearages for peacekeeping and the regular budget as well as stay on course with future dues.

Savings
By pushing for further reductions in the U.N. Secretariat's staff as well as in the administrative arms of the multilateral development organizations and financial institutions, the United States might ulti-

---

[18] See George Soros, Chairman, Independent Task Force, *American National Interest and the United Nations* (New York: Council on Foreign Relations, 1996).

mately save $100 million in annual spending. Real funding for U.N. administration in 2000 will remain twice as high as in 1970 (even after "no growth budgets" will have cut real spending power relative to today's levels; see figure 10). Even allowing for some justifiable increases in staff work in areas such as peacekeeping and arms control, and an increase in the number of member states of roughly 50 percent since 1970, the current budget seems excessive.[19] The fact that support staff outnumber professional staff by more than two to one provides further evidence of the need for change.

SUMMARY AND CALL TO POLITICAL ACTION

IN SUMMARY, these considerations together suggest that a net increase of nearly $2 billion a year above and beyond the 1997 spending level is needed in the U.S. international discretionary account. Overall spending should go up to about $21 billion in 1998 and gradually rise to about $23 billion by 2002. Budget authority should be about $22 billion in 1998 and be adjusted for inflation thereafter as well.

For those who think it unrealistic to spare international programs from cuts at a time when domestic programs are experiencing severe fiscal pressures, table 1 may be worth reviewing. International spending has already declined by about 15 percent, in real terms, this decade, and under the president's budget will be 26 percent lower in real terms in 2002 than it was in 1990. Domestic discretionary spending, by contrast, has increased more than 20 percent this decade; even factoring in the cuts now anticipated over the next few years, in 2002 it will remain 12 percent greater than it was in 1990 (and roughly equal to its 1980 real level). Entitlement programs, for their part, are growing by large percentages. There is no defensible basis for this disproportionate reduction in international affairs spending given the ongoing challenges and opportunities of the global setting in which the United States finds itself today.

---

[19] For a similar opinion, see Jesse Helms, "Saving the U.N.," *Foreign Affairs,* vol. 75, no. 5 (September/October 1996), p. 5.

The amount of increase proposed here constitutes only about 0.1 percent of total federal spending and less than 0.4 percent of all discretionary spending. It would still leave international outlays below their 1990 level in the year 2002. Despite the push for fiscal balance, all other types of federal spending besides defense will go up in real terms, under the president's plan, over the 1990-2002 period.

Some may agree with these arguments but worry about the domestic political fallout from actively supporting international spending. Indeed, few elections are won by championing foreign aid, and some may be lost that way (although the evidence is far from clear). But no poll suggests that Americans think spending one percent of the federal budget on foreign assistance and diplomacy is excessive. Some polls, such as those by Steven Kull at the University of Maryland, suggest that Americans would support spending significantly more than one percent on international assistance and related activities; others show that they would at a minimum like to sustain the current level. Americans do tend to oppose present foreign aid levels—but primarily because they believe them to be at least 10 times higher than they actually are.

Who is to do the educating, the correcting of such misperceptions, that is probably the most important prerequisite for reestablishing general public support for overseas activities? The clear answer is that it must be the president.

The president's opportunities and responsibilities in foreign policy extend beyond the fact that he has the country's only true bully pulpit. He also has predominant legal and constitutional powers in this arena. The powers of Congress, by contrast, are rather limited. (And whatever one's views of the federal government's proper role in domestic affairs, it is the only institution legally competent to conduct U.S. foreign policy.)

Although Congress has a very important role in international affairs, only the president is in the end really rewarded (or blamed) for U.S. foreign policy. He is also the only official who, as commander in chief of the country's military, has to make the most momentous decisions about using armed force when our diplomatic and economic tools of foreign policy fail. He is therefore the only person who can ultimately be expected to accept primary responsibility for this task.

In addition, as a practical budgetary matter Congress rarely adds money to the president's request for international funding. Whether at the rhetorical, political, or budgetary level, this job is one that the president must take on if it is to get done.

In practical terms, he should do three things. First, he should ask for adequate resources from Congress in his official budget request for 1998 and beyond. Second, he should convene a meeting with congressional leaders to discuss foreign affairs resources and to hammer out a broad and enduring agreement. Third, he must take the case for adequate funding to the people.

But others must be prepared to help him once he engages. Without the active support and assistance of the congressional leadership on both sides of the aisle, the issue will become partisan. At that point, opponents of foreign aid and international spending will probably gain the upper hand, given the public's misperceptions about the cost of those activities and concerns about possible cuts in domestic programs.

With united political leadership, however, Americans' best qualities can be tapped, in building the foundation for a safe and prosperous future for themselves and others, and the country can be equipped with the resources necessary for a 21st-century foreign policy that serves those goals.

February 12, 1997

PRESIDENT BILL CLINTON, STATE OF THE UNION ADDRESS EXCERPT, FEBRUARY 4, 1997

TO PREPARE America for the 21st century we must master the forces of change in the world and keep American leadership strong and sure for an uncharted time.

Fifty years ago, a farsighted America led in creating the institutions that secured victory in the Cold War and built a growing world economy. As a result, today more people than ever embrace our ideals and share our interests. Already, we have dismantled many of the blocs and barriers that divided our parents' world. For the first time, more people live under democracy than dictatorship, including every nation in our own hemisphere, but one—and its day, too, will come.

Now, we stand at another moment of change and choice—and another time to be farsighted, to bring America 50 more years of security and prosperity. In this endeavor, our first task is to help to build, for the first time, an undivided, democratic Europe. When Europe is stable, prosperous and at peace, America is more secure.

To that end, we must expand NATO by 1999, so that countries that were once our adversaries can become our allies. At the special NATO summit this summer, that is what we will begin to do. We must strengthen NATO's Partnership for Peace with non-member allies. And we must build a stable partnership between NATO and a democratic Russia. An expanded NATO is good for America. And a Europe in which all democracies define their future not in terms of what they can do to each other, but in terms of what they can do together for the good of all—that kind of Europe is good for America.

Second, America must look to the East no less than to the West. Our security demands it. Americans fought three wars in Asia in this century. Our prosperity requires it. More than two million American jobs depend upon trade with Asia.

There, too, we are helping to shape an Asian Pacific community of cooperation, not conflict. Let our progress there not mask the peril that remains. Together with South Korea, we must advance peace talks with North Korea and bridge the Cold War's last divide. And I call on Congress to fund our share of the agreement under which North Korea must continue to freeze and then dismantle its nuclear weapons program.

We must pursue a deeper dialogue with China—for the sake of our interests and our ideals. An isolated China is not good for America. A China playing its proper role in the world is. I will go to China, and I have invited China's president to come here, not because we agree on everything, but because engaging China is the best way to work on our common challenges like ending nuclear testing, and to deal frankly with our fundamental differences like human rights.

The American people must prosper in the global economy. We've worked hard to tear down trade barriers abroad so that we can create good jobs at home. I am proud to say that today, America is once again the most competitive nation and the number one exporter in the world.

Now we must act to expand our exports, especially to Asia and Latin America—two of the fastest growing regions on Earth—or be left behind as these emerging economies forge new ties with other nations. That is why we need the authority now to conclude new trade agreements that open markets to our goods and services even as we preserve our values.

We need not shrink from the challenge of the global economy. After all, we have the best workers and the best products. In a truly open market, we can out-compete anyone, anywhere on Earth.

But this is about more than economics. By expanding trade, we can advance the cause of freedom and democracy around the world. There is no better example of this truth than Latin America, where democracy and open markets are on the march together. That is why I will visit there in the spring to reinforce our important tie.

We should all be proud that America led the effort to rescue our neighbor, Mexico, from its economic crises. And we should all be proud that last month Mexico repaid the United States—three full years ahead of schedule—with half a billion dollar profit to us.

America must continue to be an unrelenting force for peace— from the Middle East to Haiti, from Northern Ireland to Africa. Taking reasonable risks for peace keeps us from being drawn into far more costly conflicts later.

With American leadership, the killing has stopped in Bosnia. Now the habits of peace must take hold. The new NATO force will allow reconstruction and reconciliation to accelerate. Tonight, I ask Congress to continue its strong support for our troops. They are doing a remarkable job there for America, and America must do right by them.

Fifth, we must move strongly against new threats to our security. In the past four years, we agreed to ban—we led the way to a worldwide agreement to ban nuclear testing. With Russia, we dramatically cut nuclear arsenals and we stopped targeting each other's citizens. We are acting to prevent nuclear materials from falling into the wrong hands and to rid the world of land mines. We are working with other nations with renewed intensity to fight drug traffickers and to stop terrorists before they act, and hold them fully accountable if they do.

Now, we must rise to a new test of leadership: ratifying the Chemical Weapons Convention. (Applause.) Make no mistake about it, it will make our troops safer from chemical attack; it will help us to fight terrorism. We have no more important obligations—especially in the wake of what we now know about the Gulf War. This treaty has been bipartisan from the beginning—supported by Republican and Democratic administrations and Republican and Democratic members of Congress—and already approved by 68 nations.

But if we do not act by April the 29th—when this Convention goes into force, with or without us—we will lose the chance to have Americans leading and enforcing this effort. Together we must make the Chemical Weapons Convention law, so that at last we can begin to outlaw poison gas from the Earth.

Finally, we must have the tools to meet all these challenges. We must maintain a strong and ready military. We must increase funding for weapons modernization by the year 2000, and we must take good care of our men and women in uniform. They are the world's finest.

We must also renew our commitment to America's diplomacy, and pay our debts and dues to international financial institutions like the World Bank, and to a reforming United Nations. (Applause.) Every dollar we devote to preventing conflicts, to promoting democracy, to stopping the spread of disease and starvation, brings a sure return in security and savings. Yet international affairs spending today is just one percent of the federal budget—a small fraction of what America invested in diplomacy to choose leadership over escapism at the start of the Cold War. If America is to continue to lead the world, we here who lead America simply must find the will to pay our way.

A farsighted America moved the world to a better place over these last 50 years. And so it can be for another 50 years. But a shortsighted America will soon find its words falling on deaf ears all around the world.

Almost exactly 50 years ago, in the first winter of the Cold War, President Truman stood before a Republican Congress and called upon our country to meet its responsibilities of leadership. This was his warning—he said, "If we falter, we may endanger the peace of the world, and we shall surely endanger the welfare of this nation." That Congress, led by Republicans like Senator Arthur Vandenberg, answered President Truman's call. Together, they made the commitments that strengthened our country for 50 years.

Now let us do the same. Let us do what it takes to remain the indispensable nation—to keep America strong, secure and prosperous for another 50 years.

EXCERPTS FROM THE FISCAL 1998 PRESIDENTIAL BUDGET PROPOSAL

9. Supporting America's Global Leadership

The challenge before us plainly is two-fold—to seize the opportunities for more people to enjoy peace and freedom, security and prosperity, and to move strongly and swiftly against the dangers that change has produced.

President Clinton
September 24, 1996

THIS BUDGET fully supports America's global leadership and advances our national goals—protecting our vital strategic interests and expanding the reach of democratic governance, ensuring our influence in the international community, promoting sustainable development and the expansion of free markets and American exports, and responding to new international problems and humanitarian emergencies that can undermine our security.

Table 9-1. INTERNATIONAL DISCRETIONARY PROGRAMS
(Budget authority, $ millions)

	1993 Actual	1997 Estimate[1]	1998 Proposed	2002 Proposed	Percent Change: 1993 to 1997	Percent Change: 1997 to 2002
International development and humanitarian assistance	8,900	6,644	7,712	6,978	-25%	+5%
International security assistance	6,148	5,928	5,959	6,041	-4%	+2%
Conduct of foreign affairs	4,300	3,890	4,164	4,026	-10%	+3%
Foreign information and exchange activities	1,247	1,098	1,087	1,070	-12%	-3%
International financial programs ...	12,662	549	4,052	647	-96%	+18%
IMF programs	(12,063)	...	(3,521)	...	NA	NA
Total, International discretionary programs	**33,257**	**18,109**	**22,974**	**18,762**	**-46%**	**+4%**
Total, excluding IMF programs ..	**21,194**	**18,109**	**19,453**	**18,762**	**-15%**	**+4%**

NA = Not applicable.

[1]Consistent with changes in the 1996 Farm Bill, the P.L. 480 Title I direct credit program has been reclassified from International Affairs programs to Agriculture programs starting in 1996.

Protecting America's key strategic interests remains a timeless goal of our diplomacy. As we move toward the 21st Century, we have a great opportunity to expand the scope of democracy, further ensuring that our interests remain unthreatened. Facing the dilemmas of peacekeeping, regional crises, and economic change, the international community needs the United States as a leader and a full partner, meeting its international commitments. Advancing U.S. interests in a global economy brings expanded missions to our diplomacy and trade strategy. A less-orderly world also creates new challenges to our security—from regional and ethnic conflicts, the proliferation of weapons of mass destruction, international terrorism and crime, narcotics, and environmental degradation.

With such a broad agenda for leadership, America must not withdraw into isolationism and protectionism or fail to provide the resources required to carry out this mission. The budget proposes $19.5 billion for ongoing international affairs programs. While this request is seven percent above the 1997 level, it constitutes only slightly over one percent of the budget and 0.25 percent of Gross Domestic Product.

PROTECTING AMERICAN SECURITY AND PROMOTING DEMOCRACY

The first goal of America's international strategy must be to promote and protect our interests in regions that historically have been critical to our security. The Administration's record is encouraging. Through skilled diplomacy, the judicious use of military force, and carefully targeted bilateral and multilateral economic assistance, the United States has advanced the peace process in Europe and the Middle East, reducing threats to our interests in these key regions. Through diplomatic leadership, economic assistance, and trade negotiations, we have maintained our leadership in Asia. Our goals are to secure these achievements, advance the peace process, and deepen regional cooperation in the future.

Perhaps the most serious national security threat facing the Nation today hinges on the course of events over the next few years in the New Independent States (NIS) of the former Soviet Union. We have made substantial progress in helping encourage the emergence of free markets and democracy in the NIS. In particular, our relations with Russia are strong. The United States has provided unwavering support for the emergence of democracy in Russia, leading this past year to the first free presidential reelection in Russian history. Some other NIS countries are progressing more slowly toward democracy and free markets, but overall regional progress has been remarkable.

Nevertheless, the June 1996 Russian elections represent not only a success but a warning—the latter embodied in the large vote for President Yeltsin's opposition, an opposition that derived its strength from Russia's severe economic distress. The Administration believes it is absolutely critical, at this turning point, to demonstrate our continuing support for democratic reform and free markets in Russia and throughout the NIS; the ultimate success of this process is vital to our national security. Moreover, we must begin to shape our assistance program in ways that support the mature trade and investment relationship that is starting to emerge between the United States and the countries in this region. Thus, the budget proposes $900 million for NIS funding, a 44-percent increase over 1997. The increase includes a Partnership for Freedom initiative, designed to initiate a new phase of U.S. engagement with NIS countries focused on trade and investment, long-term cooperative activities, and partnerships.

The region at the heart of the Cold War conflict—Central Europe—has made enormous progress toward institutionalizing free markets and democracy. It is no longer a threat to American and European security; it is starting to be a partner in the transatlantic community. The economies of the Northern tier countries, such as Poland, the Czech Republic, and Hungary, are largely free and privatized; they are moving from direct assistance, which soon they will no longer require, to significant economic integration with the United States and Western Europe. At the same time, countries in this region are reshaping their security relationships with the West as they move toward potential membership in NATO.

Central European countries in the Southern tier also have made great progress. U.S. leadership has been critical in ending the bloody hostilities in Bosnia, establishing new governments through free elections, and beginning economic reconstruction. The pace of reconciliation and recovery remains gradual, and the need for continued American leadership is great. The other countries in the southern part of this region also look to the United States to remain committed to their struggle to create democratic governments and free, open markets.

The budget proposes to increase funding for economic assistance in Central Europe to $492 million—including the final $200 million installment on the U.S. commitment to Bosnian reconstruction. While programs for the Northern tier are phasing down, we must continue to support implementation of the Dayton Peace Accords and to sustain the emergence of free market democracies in the Southern tier. In addition, the budget seeks to increase support for foreign military financing for the countries of Central and Eastern Europe through the President's Partnership for Peace initiative, which will facilitate their efforts to meet the conditions for membership in NATO.

Our strategic interest in peace in the Middle East is as strong as ever. The peace process has achieved much already. The need for reconciliation remains urgent, and America continues to play a leadership role in the effort to craft a durable, comprehensive regional peace. The budget proposes $5.3 billion for military financing grants and economic support to sustain the Middle East peace process. The proposed increase of nearly $100 million includes $52.5 million for an initial U.S. contribution for the Bank for Economic Cooperation and Development in the Middle East and North Africa, which will play a key role in promoting regional economic integration. The budget also provides additional security assistance to Jordan, recognizing that country's needs and its important contribution to the peace process.

The rest of our economic and security assistance programs are designed to support peace and democracy in countries and regions where our leadership has helped those processes emerge: consolidating democratic gains in Haiti; supporting reconciliation and peace in Guatemala and Cambodia; and strengthening the capacity of African governments to provide regional peacekeeping on that troubled continent.

Financing America's Leadership

ENSURING AMERICA'S LEADERSHIP
IN THE INTERNATIONAL COMMUNITY

Following World War II, the United States assumed a unique leadership role in building international institutions to bring the world's nations together to meet mutual security and economic needs. It took an alliance to win the war, and it clearly would take an alliance to ensure the peace. We sponsored and provided significant funding for the United Nations, the International Monetary Fund, and the World Bank, along with specialized and regional security and financial institutions that became the foundation of international cooperation during the Cold War.

To ensure financial stability for this international community, the members of many of these organizations entered into treaties or similar instruments committing them to pay shares (or "assessments") of the organizations' budgets. Congress ratified these agreements, making them binding on us. For international financial institutions, like the World Bank and its regional partners, the United States has made firm commitments to regular replenishments, subject to the congressional authorization and appropriations processes.

Now, America's leadership in this international institutional network is threatened. In recent years, Congress has not fully appropriated the funds needed to meet the treaty-bound assessments of international organizations or our commitments to the multilateral banks. As a result, U.S. arrears now total over $1 billion to the United Nations and other organizations, much of it for peacekeeping operations, and over $850 million to financial institutions. Congress has raised some legitimate concerns about how these organizations operate, but America's failure to meet its obligations has undercut our efforts to achieve reforms on which the Administration and Congress agree. Today, our ability to lead, especially in the process of institutional reform, is being seriously undermined.

The Administration believes that we must end the stalemate this year—and that we can do so consistent with our goal of institutional reform. With new leadership in the United Nations, we have a unique opportunity. The budget proposes to fully fund the 1998 assessments for the United Nations, affiliated organizations, and peacekeeping, and to pay $100 million of our arrears. It also seeks a one-time, $921 million advance appropriation for the balance of U.N. and related organization arrears, to become available in 1999. The release of these appropriated arrears would depend on the adoption of a series of reforms in the coming year, specific to each organization, that should reduce the annual amount that we must pay these organizations, starting with their next biennial budgets. These reforms would include a reduction in the U.S. share of organizational budgets, management reforms yielding lower organizational budgets, and the elimination of, or U.S. withdrawal from, low-priority programs and organizations.

The Administration wants to work closely with Congress to shape this package, lowering out-year funding requirements while maintaining strong U.S. leadership in organizations and programs important to our national interests. Enacting the advance appropriation is an essential step in achieving these objectives. It would show that we recognize our legal obligations and are determined to maintain the sanctity of our treaty commitments as we press for changes in the organizations. It would give us the leverage to mobilize support from other nations for the reforms we seek and for the lowering of our future assessments. Failure to arrive at an agreed-upon solution this year will put U.S. international leadership at risk in the next century.

We are equally committed to restoring our leadership in, and reforming, the multilateral development banks (MDBs). Our commitments to them represent America's full-faith pledge. Moreover, the MDBs already have undertaken significant reforms in response to Administration and congressional concerns, including cuts in administrative expenses. The budget would eliminate our arrears over the next three years while meeting ongoing commitments that were negotiated down by 40 percent from previous funding agreements. The budget also includes funds to eliminate all arrears to the World Bank's International Development Association affiliate that lends to the world's poorest countries, many of them in Africa. Future budgets would seek to eliminate all of the arrears, while continuing our success in lowering the level of future U.S. commitments.

Our leadership in international institutions also has been critical in preventing international financial crises. As the Mexican peso crisis demonstrated, the increased interdependence of our trading and monetary systems means that a monetary crisis in any major trading nation affects all nations. Consequently, the G-10 nations and a number of other current and emerging economic powers have negotiated the New Arrangements to Borrow (NAB), in order to provide a credit line for the International Monetary Fund (IMF) in cases when a monetary crises in any country could threaten the stability of the international monetary system. The budget proposes a one-time appropriation of $3.5 billion in budget authority for the U.S. share, but it will not count as an outlay or increase the deficit; the United States will receive an increase in its international reserve assets that corresponds to any transfer to the IMF under the NAB.

PROMOTING AN OPEN TRADING SYSTEM

The Administration remains committed to opening global markets and integrating the global economic system, which has become a key element of continuing economic prosperity here at home. Achieving this goal is increasingly central to our global diplomatic activities. We are helping to lay the groundwork for sustained, non-inflationary growth into the next century by implementing the North American Free Trade Agreement and the multilateral trade agreements concluded during the Uruguay Round. We are conducting a vigorous follow-up to ensure that we receive the full benefit of these agreements. At the December 1996 World Trade Organization ministerial meeting in Singapore, for example, negotiators reached agreement on lowering many of the remaining barriers to trade in information technology, which will significantly benefit U.S. firms and workers. We are finalizing our anti-dumping and countervailing duty regulations, which implement commitments made in the Uruguay Round.

To promote other, mutually-beneficial trade relationships, the Administration will propose legislation for "fast-track" authority to negotiate greater trade liberalization.[1] It also will propose to extend the

---

[1] Fast track is a procedure designed to expedite congressional approval of trade agreements between the United States and other nations.

authorization of the Generalized System of Preferences for developing countries beyond its current expiration date of May 31, 1997 and to give the eligible countries of the Caribbean Basin Initiative expanded trade benefits.

We are more closely integrating the Government's trade promotion activities through the Trade Promotion Coordinating Committee (TPCC), creating a synergy among agency trade programs that will significantly improve American business' ability to win contracts overseas, and creating export-related jobs at home. The budget puts a high priority on programs that help U.S. exporters meet foreign competition, and TPCC agencies are developing rigorous performance measures to help ensure that programs in this area are effective.

As discussed earlier in this chapter, U.S. assistance is important in encouraging the emergence of free market economies in Central Europe and the NIS, where our programs increasingly focus on facilitating a mature trade and investment relationship with the United States.

Over time, our bilateral development assistance, provided through the U.S. Agency for International Development (USAID), likewise promotes the emergence of growing market economies in developing countries by supporting market-friendly policies and key institutions. Economic growth and market-oriented policy reforms in the developing world create growing demand for U.S. goods and services as well as investment opportunities for U.S. businesses. On a larger scale, the multilateral development banks also promote economic growth and increased demand for our exports. The budget proposes that our bilateral development assistance and contributions to the multilateral development banks grow by 25 percent—from $2.6 billion to $3.3 billion.

Three smaller agencies provide U.S. Government financial support for American exports. The Export-Import Bank is a principal source of export assistance, offering loans, loan guarantees, and insurance for exports, primarily of capital goods. To assure that its programs operate as economically as possible, the Bank is considering raising some fees, thereby lowering net spending in 1998 while maintaining a strong overall level of export support. The Overseas Private Investment Corporation (OPIC) provides political risk insurance for, and finances, U.S. investment in developing countries, leading to greater U.S. exports. The budget proposes to maintain 1998 OPIC funding close to the 1997 level. The Trade and Development Agency (TDA) makes grants for feasibility studies of capital projects abroad; subsequent implementation of these projects can generate exports of U.S. goods and services. The budget increases funding for TDA over the 1997 level. With the new emphasis on trade and investment in the NIS, the Export-Import Bank, OPIC, and TDA may well become important channels for further funding directed at this region.

Along with the Government's financial support for U.S. exports, the Commerce Department's International Trade Administration (ITA) promotes U.S. trade through its network of Export Assistance Centers and overseas offices. These centers and offices provide export counseling to the American sector. The budget proposes a slight increase for ITA compared to 1997.

LEADING THE RESPONSE TO NEW INTERNATIONAL CHALLENGES

Another fundamental goal of our international leadership, and an increasing focus of our diplomacy, is meeting the new transnational threats to U.S. and global security—the proliferation of weapons of mass destruction, drug trafficking and the spread of crime and terrorism on an international scale, unrestrained population growth, and environmental degradation. We also must sustain our leadership in meeting the continuing challenge of refugee flows and natural and human-made disasters.

In 1997, the Administration will seek Senate ratification of the Comprehensive Test Ban Treaty and the Chemical Weapons Convention, both critical to our long-term security and to preventing the spread of weapons of mass destruction. The budget supports the implementation of these agreements. U.S. diplomacy and law enforcement activities are playing a key role in preventing the spread of such weapons to outlaw states such as Libya, Iraq, Iran, Syria, and North Korea. The Defense Department's Nunn-Lugar program and the State Department's Nonproliferation and Disarmament Fund help support these efforts. (For more information on the Nunn-Lugar program, see Chapter 10.) In addition, U.S. support for such organizations as the International Atomic Energy Agency and the Korean Peninsula Energy Development Organization is critical to meeting our non-proliferation goals.

U.S. bilateral assistance programs are also critical to tackling other important transnational problems. Our international counter-narcotics efforts are making real progress in drug-producing countries. After several years of deeply cutting the Administration's budget requests for counter-narcotics purposes, Congress provided the full requested amount for 1997, permitting the United States to intensify its efforts to curb cocaine production in the Andean countries by offering growers attractive economic alternatives. The budget proposes $230 million for the State Department's narcotics and anti-crime programs, eight percent more than in 1997, with most of the increase focussed on programs in Peru.

In addition, USAID development assistance and U.S. contributions to international efforts, such as the Global Environment Facility, support large and successful programs to improve the environment and reduce population growth. The United States is the recognized world leader in promoting safe and effective family planning projects.

Disasters, humanitarian crises, and refugee flows are certain to remain central challenges to our leadership. The budget continues our historically strong commitment to refugee and disaster relief, proposing $1.7 billion, which sustains these programs at the 1997 level. This assistance, which reflects the humanitarian spirit of all Americans, has long enjoyed bipartisan support.

CONDUCTING FOREIGN AFFAIRS

An effective American diplomacy is the critical foundation for meeting our foreign policy goals. The budget supports a strong U.S. presence at over 250 embassies and other posts overseas, promoting U.S. interests abroad and protecting and serving Americans by providing consular services. These activities include the basic work of diplomacy—the reporting, analysis, and negotiations that often go unnoticed but that allow us to anticipate and prevent threats to our national security as well as discover new opportunities to promote American interests. The budget proposes $2.7 billion for the State Department to maintain its worldwide operations, modernize its information technology and communications systems, and accommodate security and facility requirements at posts abroad.

The budget also proposes two significant innovations in State Department management.

- One would make about $600 million in immigration, passport, and other fees, which now go to the Treasury Department, available to finance State Department operations directly. Improvements in how these State Department operations perform will, thus, be directly linked to the receipts they generate.
- The other innovation restructures the management of the diplomatic platform to support the overseas activities of other Federal agencies. This reform recognizes the magnitude of the State Department's overseas administrative workload, the need to carry it out efficiently, and the need to allocate the costs of overseas support fairly among agencies. With approval of the President's Management Council, the various agencies represented abroad have designed a new overseas administrative arrangement—the International Cooperative Administrative Support Services program. The Administration will propose to fund this new arrangement in a budget amendment that it will send to Congress shortly after transmitting the budget.

13. International Affairs

THE INTERNATIONAL AFFAIRS function, for which the Administration proposes $23 billion for 1998, encompasses a wide range of activities that advance American interests through diplomacy, foreign assistance, support for American exports, and the activities of international organizations. Certain tax provisions also support Amer-

Table 13-1. FEDERAL RESOURCES IN SUPPORT OF INTERNATIONAL AFFAIRS

(In millions of dollars)

Function 150	1996 Actual	Estimate					
		1997	1998	1999	2000	2001	2002
Spending:							
Discretionary Budget Authority	18,122	18,109	22,974	20,079	19,095	18,811	18,762
Mandatory Outlays:							
Existing law	-4,840	-4,744	-4,433	-3,963	-3,839	-3,655	-3,487
Proposed legislation	......	......	......	37	......	......	......
Credit Activity:							
Direct loan disbursements ..	1,674	2,150	1,900	2,191	2,162	2,013	2,023
Guaranteed loans	8,418	12,692	12,059	13,093	13,736	13,702	14,000
Tax Expenditures:							
Existing law	6,520	6,980	7,565	8,165	8,790	9,445	10,125
Proposed legislation	......	10	-820	-1,408	-1,484	-1,674	-1,773

ican business. The conduct of foreign relations is inherently a governmental function, which explains the need for sustained Government activity and budgetary support.

DIPLOMACY

The State Department and its overseas operations are at the heart of international affairs activities and programs, and they consume $2.7 billion, or 14 percent, of the resources. These funds finance the salaries and related operating expenses of the Foreign Service and other Department personnel, and the costs of overseas facilities. The Department carries out foreign policy planning and oversight in Washington, conducts diplomacy, and represents the United States at over 250 overseas embassies and other posts. Overseas posts also provide administrative support to about 25 other Federal departments and agencies.

The major achievement of American diplomacy over the past half century was creating and sustaining the alliances, notably NATO, that successfully countered the Soviet bloc's threat to world security. More recently, diplomatic objectives include establishing viable democracies in formerly totalitarian countries such as in Eastern Europe and the former Soviet Union, curbing regional instability in areas of importance to U.S. security such as Bosnia, promoting the American economy through trade negotiations and the support of U.S. businesses, and addressing transnational issues such as the environment through multilateral and bilateral negotiations. American diplomacy also has been critical over the past 20 years in promoting peace and reconciliation in the Middle East. Finally, the Department has the continuing responsibility to protect and assist U.S. citizens abroad.

FOREIGN ASSISTANCE

The largest single part of international affairs spending—$13.7 billion, or 74 percent of the total—goes for a wide variety of overseas assistance programs traditionally categorized as security assistance, development aid, and humanitarian assistance.

Security Assistance: International Security Assistance comes mainly through the Foreign Military Financing program (FMF, which the State Department oversees and the Defense Security Assistance Agency manages) and the Economic Support Fund (ESF, which State oversees and the U.S. Agency for International Development manages). Over the past 50 years, security aid helped support the military establishments of friendly countries, mainly around the perimeter of the Soviet Union, and helped ease the economic strain of their defense forces. On the whole, these countries played a critical role in containing the Soviet Union.

The FMF program finances the transfer of military goods and services to eligible countries, using grant funds and a small loan program. The ESF program provides only grant funding. Currently, these two programs devote an overwhelming share of their resources to supporting the Middle East peace process. For a number of years, over $5 billion a year has gone for this purpose. This funding demonstrates strong U.S. support for the actions that regional leaders are taking to advance the peace process. Most of the remaining funds support the transition of Eastern European countries to NATO membership, the establishment of democracy in countries such as Angola, Cambodia and Haiti, and the training of foreign military personnel, primarily from developing countries.

Development Assistance: Development assistance is carried out through a range of programs:

• The Treasury Department manages contributions to multilateral development banks. A major portion of them support the World Bank group of institutions, which make development loans both at near-market rates and on highly-concessional terms, and which provide financing and investment insurance for private sector activity in the developing world. Contributions also go to four regional development banks for Africa, Asia, Europe (lending to Eastern Europe and the New Independent States of the former Soviet Union), and Latin America. All but the European bank have concessional loan programs. Two special programs also receive U.S. contributions: the Global Environment Facility, which supports environmental activities related to development projects; and the North American Development Bank, which was established in conjunction with the North American Free Trade Agreement and which supports environmental projects along the U.S.-Mexican border.

• The bilateral development assistance programs of the U.S. Agency for International Development (USAID) target five sectors: broad-based economic growth, population (for which the United States is the leading donor worldwide), health, the environment, and democracy building. In recent years, USAID has significantly restructured its program to focus on countries most likely to adopt economic reforms, in order to encourage free markets along with improvements in democratic governance. USAID has developed performance measures to help it allocate resources, and has made major internal management reforms to improve its effectiveness and cut costs.

• State, USAID, and other agencies (the U.S. Information Agency, Export-Import Bank, Peace Corps, and Overseas Private Investment Corporation) also carry out grant and lending programs similar to development assistance to support the transition to free market democracy in Central Europe and the New Independent States.

Encouraging economic development has proved a difficult task, requiring far more time for success than policymakers assumed in the early 1960s when they initiated many of the current programs. Nevertheless, a number of developing countries have shifted from grants and highly concessional loans to near-market rate loans, and a few countries have graduated from the ranks of foreign assistance recipients. Some early recipients of U.S. bilateral assistance in East Asia are now among the world's most dynamic economies, and the major Latin American countries no longer require large-scale grant aid.

Humanitarian Assistance: Humanitarian assistance programs also encompass various activities:

- USAID manages two food aid programs under Public Law 480, first enacted in 1954. The agency makes humanitarian food donations, under Title II of the law, through U.S. voluntary agencies and the United Nations World Food Program, and directly to foreign governments. Depending on the circumstances each year, about half of this program goes to disaster relief—with recent large donations in such areas as central Africa and Bosnia—and half to longer-term development projects. Under Title III, USAID provides food to governments that sell it, then use the proceeds to carry out agricultural reforms.
- State and USAID also manage funds for refugee support and disaster assistance. State manages humanitarian refugee relief funding—mainly grants to international agencies such as the United Nations High Commissioner for Refugees and the International Committee of the Red Cross. USAID manages the Office of Foreign Disaster Assistance, which provides grants to deal with natural and human disasters overseas. In a crisis, these two programs and Title II of Public Law 480 are closely coordinated.

The United States continues to lead the world in responding to humanitarian crises, due to Americans' support for such assistance and U.S. voluntary agencies' unequaled capacity to implement relief programs quickly and effectively. This humane concern and excellent program delivery has, over the years, countered world food shortages, alleviated the impact of major droughts in particular countries, managed surges of refugees, and dealt with man-made disasters such as genocide in Rwanda.

EXPORT PROMOTION

While U.S. diplomacy and foreign assistance promote open markets and export opportunities for U.S. business, three other international affairs agencies more directly support or finance American exports. The Export-Import Bank provides short- and long-term loans and loan guarantees and insurance to support U.S. exports, primarily exports of capital goods. Bank support is designed to remedy imperfections in private capital markets, and to counter financing by the official export credit agencies of other countries. The Overseas Private Investment Corporation provides loans, guarantees, and insurance for U.S. business investment overseas. The Trade and Development Agency provides grant financing for feasibility studies on major infrastructure and other development projects abroad. These agencies' activities generate considerable payoffs for U.S. exports.

A series of tax preferences also benefit U.S. trade activities. Americans working abroad, for example, often may exclude $70,000 of income and a portion of their housing costs from taxes. In addition, U.S. exporters who work through Foreign Sales Corporations may exempt significant portions of their income from U.S. taxes. U.S. exporters also may allocate more of their earnings abroad (and thereby reduce their tax obligations). Finally, earnings from U.S.-controlled foreign corporations benefit from a tax deferral—they are not subject to U.S. taxes until they are received by U.S. shareholders as dividends or other distributions.

INTERNATIONAL ORGANIZATIONS

The United States promotes its foreign policy goals through a wide variety of international organizations, to which it makes both assessed and voluntary contributions. While our global leadership is most clear in the United Nations, other organizations are important to U.S. interests.

The International Atomic Energy Agency, for example, strongly supports America's non-proliferation goals, while the World Health Organization pursues our goal of eradicating disease. NATO advances our national security goals in Europe. We support our development assistance goals as a leading contributor to the United Nations Development Program. Finally, our assessed contributions to U.N.-supported peacekeeping operations, and our voluntary contributions to such peacekeeping efforts as the Multilateral Force in the Sinai, support peace-keeping in regions that are important to our interests.

STATEMENT BY SECRETARY OF STATE-DESIGNATE
MADELEINE K. ALBRIGHT

*Excerpted from January 8, 1997, Senate Foreign Relations
Committee Confirmation Hearing*

WE HAVE REACHED a point more than halfway between the disintegration of the Soviet Union and the start of a new century. Our nation is respected and at peace. Our alliances are vigorous. Our economy is strong. And from the distant corners of Asia, to the merging democracies of Central Europe and Africa, to the community of democracies that exists within our own hemisphere—and to the one impermanent exception to that community, Castro's Cuba—American institutions and ideals are a model for those who have, or who aspire to, freedom.

All this is no accident, and its continuation is by no means inevitable. Democratic progress must be sustained as it was built—by American leadership. And our leadership must be sustained if our interests are to be protected around the world.

Do not doubt, those interests are not geopolitical abstractions, they are real. It matters to our children whether they grow up in a world where the dangers posed by weapons of mass destruction have been minimized or allowed to run out of control. It matters to the millions of Americans who work, farm or invest whether the global economy continues to create good new jobs and open new markets, or whether—through miscalculation or protectionism—it begins to spiral downward. It matters to our families whether illegal drugs continue to pour into our neighborhoods from overseas. It matters to Americans who travel abroad or go about their daily business at home whether the scourge of international terrorism is reduced. It matters to our workers and businesspeople whether they will be unfairly forced to compete against companies that violate fair labor standards, despoil the environment or gain contracts not through competition but corruption. And it matters to us all whether through inattention or indifference, we allow small wars to grow into large ones that put our safety and freedom at risk.

To defeat the dangers and seize the opportunities, we must be more than audience, more even than actors, we must be the authors of the history of our age. A half century ago, after the devastation caused by Depression, holocaust and war, it was not enough to say that what we were against had failed. Leaders such as Truman, Marshall and Vandenberg were determined to build a lasting peace. And together with our allies, they forged a set of institutions that would defend freedom, rebuild economies, uphold law and preserve peace.

Today, it is not enough for us to say that Communism has failed. We must continue building a new framework—adapted to the demands of a new century—that will protect our citizens and our friends; reinforce our values; and secure our future. In so doing, we must direct our energies, not as our predecessors did, against a single virulent ideology. We face a variety of threats, some as old as ethnic conflict; some as new as letter bombs; some as long-term as global warming; some as dangerous as nuclear weapons falling into the wrong hands.

To cope with such a variety of threats, we will need a full range of foreign policy tools. That is why our armed forces must remain the best-led, best-trained, best-equipped and most respected in the world. And as President Clinton has pledged, and our military leaders ensure, they will.

It is also why we need first-class diplomacy. Force, and the credible possibility of its use, are essential to defend our vital interests and to keep America safe. But force alone can be a blunt instrument, and there are many problems it cannot solve. To be effective, force and diplomacy must complement and reinforce each other. For there will be many occasions, in many places, where we will rely on diplomacy to protect our interests, and we will expect our diplomats to defend those interests with skill, knowledge and spine.

If confirmed, one of my most important tasks will be to work with Congress to ensure that we have the superb diplomatic representation that our people deserve and our interests demand. We cannot have that on the cheap. We must invest the resources needed to maintain American leadership. Consider the stakes. We are talking here about one percent of our federal budget, but that one percent may well determine fifty percent of the history that is written about our era.

Unfortunately, as Senator Lugar recently pointed out, currently, "our international operations are underfunded and understaffed." He noted, as well, that not only our interests, but our efforts to balance the budget would be damaged if American disengagement were to result in "nuclear terrorism, a trade war, an energy crisis, a major regional conflict . . . or some other preventable disaster."

Mr. Chairman, we are the world's richest, strongest, most respected nation. We are also the largest debtor to the United Nations and the international financial institutions. We provide a smaller percentage of our wealth to support democracy and growth in the developing world than any other industrialized nation. And over the past four years, the Department of State has cut more than 2000 employees, downgraded positions, closed more than 30 embassies or consulates, and deferred badly-needed modernization of infrastructure and communications. We have also suffered a 30 percent reduction in our foreign assistance programs since 1991. It is said that we have moved from an era where the big devour the small to an era where the fast devour the slow. If that is the case, your State Department, with its obsolete technology, $300 million in deferred maintenance and a shrinking base of skilled personnel, is in trouble.

If confirmed, I will strive to fulfill my obligation to manage our foreign policy effectively and efficiently. I will work with this Committee and the Congress to ensure that the American public gets full value for each tax dollar spent. But I will also want to ensure that our foreign policy successfully promotes and protects the interests of the American people. In addition, I will want to work with you to spur continued reform and to pay our bills at the United Nations, an organization that Americans helped create, that reflects ideals that we share and that serves goals of stability, law and international cooperation that are in our interests.

The debate over adequate funding for foreign policy is not new in America. It has been joined repeatedly from the time the Continental Congress sent Ben Franklin to Paris, to the proposals for Lend Lease and the Marshall Plan that bracketed World War II, to the start of the SEED and Nunn-Lugar programs a few years ago. In each case, history has looked more kindly on those who argued for our engagement than on those who said we just could not afford to lead.

Financing America's Leadership

REMARKS BY SECRETARY OF STATE
MADELEINE K. ALBRIGHT

*Excerpted from Address at Rice Memorial Center,
Rice University, Houston, Texas, February 7, 1997*

LAST TUESDAY, in his State of the Union Address, President Clinton said that to prepare America for the 21st century, we must master the forces of change in the world and keep American leadership strong and sure for an uncharted time.

Fortunately, thanks to the President's own leadership, and that of his predecessor President George Bush—Houston's most distinguished adopted son—I begin work with the wind at my back.

Our nation is respected and at peace. Our alliances are vigorous. Our economy is strong. And from the distant corners of Asia, to the emerging democracies of Central Europe and Africa, to the community of liberty that exists within our own hemisphere, American institutions and ideals are a model for those who have, or who aspire to, freedom.

All this is no accident, and its continuation is by no means inevitable. Democratic progress must be sustained as it was built—by American leadership. And our leadership must be sustained if our interests are to be protected around the world.

That is why our armed forces must remain the best-led, best-trained, best-equipped and most respected in the world. And as President Clinton has pledged, they will.

It is also why we need first-class diplomacy. Force, and the credible possibility of its use, are essential to defend our vital interests and to keep America safe. But force alone can be a blunt instrument, and there are many problems it cannot solve.

To be effective, force and diplomacy must complement and reinforce each other. For there will be many occasions, in many places, where we will rely on diplomacy to protect our interests, and we will expect our diplomats to defend those interests with skill, knowledge and spine.

Unfortunately, in the words of Senator Richard Lugar of Indiana, our international operations today are underfunded and under-staffed. We are the world's richest and most powerful nation, but we are also the number one debtor to the U.N. and the international financial institutions. We are dead last among the industrialized nations in the percentage of our wealth that we use to promote democracy and growth in the developing world.

And diplomatically, we are steadily and unilaterally disarming ourselves. Over the past four years, the Department of State has cut more than 2000 employees, closed more than 30 overseas posts and slashed foreign assistance by almost one-third.

This trend is not acceptable. Many of you are students. Someday, one of you may occupy the office I hold and that Secretary Baker held. I hope you do. And I assure you that I will do everything I can in my time to see that you have the necessary diplomatic tools in your time to protect our nation and do your job.

Yesterday, the President submitted his budget request to Congress for the coming fiscal year. That budget, which totals some 1.8 trillion dollars, includes about $20 billion for the entire range of international affairs programs. This would pay for everything from our share of reconstruction in Bosnia to enforcing sanctions against Saddam Hussein to waging war around the world against drug kingpins and organized crime.

Approval of this budget matters, not only to me, or to those who consider themselves foreign policy experts, but to each and every one of us. For example, if you live in Houston, more than likely your job, or that of a member of your family, is linked to the health of the global economy, whether through investments, or trade, or competition from workers abroad, or from newly arrived workers here. This region's robust agricultural and energy sectors are particularly affected by overseas prices, policies and politics.

Your family, like most in America, probably has good reason to look ahead with hope. But you are also anxious. For you see crime fueled by drugs that pour across nearby borders. You see advanced technology creating not only new wonders, but new and more deadly arms. On your television screen, you see the consequences of letter bombs and poisonous serums and sudden explosions and ask yourself when and where terrorists may strike next.

Whether you are a student, or parent, or teacher, or worker, you are concerned about the future our young people will face. Will the global marketplace continue to expand and generate new opportunities and new jobs? Will our global environment survive the assault of increasing population and pollution? Will the plague of AIDS and other epidemic disease be brought under control? And will the world continue to move away from the threat of nuclear Armageddon, or will that specter once again loom large, perhaps in some altered and even more dangerous form?

If you are like most Americans, you do not think of the United States as just another country. You want America to be strong and respected. And you want that strength and respect to continue through the final years of this century and into the next.

Considering all this, one thing should be clear. The success or failure of American foreign policy is not only relevant to our lives; it will be a determining factor in the quality of our lives. It will make the difference between a future characterized by peace, rising prosperity and law, and a more uncertain future, in which our economy and security are always at risk, our peace of mind is always under assault, and American leadership is increasingly in doubt.

We are talking here about 1 percent of the federal budget; but that 1 percent may determine 50 percent of the history that is written about our era; and it will affect the lives of 100 percent of the American people.

Let me be more specific.

First, foreign policy creates jobs. The Clinton Administration has negotiated more than 200 trade agreements since 1993. Those agreements have helped exports to soar and boosted employment by more than 1.6 million. For example, earlier today I met with Mexican Foreign Minister Gurria. Our growing trade with Mexico is a genuine success story. Last year alone, 125 billion dollars in exports were traded. And with NAFTA now in place, we estimate that this coming year some 2.2 million American workers will produce goods for export to our NAFTA partners.

By passing NAFTA, concluding the Uruguay Round, and forging commitments to free trade in Latin America and Asia, we have helped create a growing global economy with America as its dynamic hub.

This matters a lot down here. Houston is one of America's great ports. Texas is our second leading exporting state. Commerce makes you grow. And there are more direct benefits. For years, Texas grains have been among the leading commodities sold through the Food for Peace Program.

America's economic expansion is no accident. It derives primarily from the genius of our scientists, the enterprise of our businesspeople and the productivity of our factories and farms. But it has been helped along by American diplomats who work to ensure that American business and labor receive fair treatment overseas.

For example, if an American businessman or woman bribes a foreign official in return for a contract, that American is fined or goes to jail. If a European bribes that same foreign official, chances are he will get a tax deduction. We are working hard to create higher standards that apply to all. And we have opened the doors of embassies around the world to U.S. entrepreneurs seeking our help in creating a level playing field for American firms and more opportunities for Americans back home.

Have no doubt, these efforts will continue. For as long as I am Secretary of State, America's diplomatic influence will be harnessed to the task of helping America's economy to grow.

We will also use diplomacy to keep America safe.

The Cold War may be over, but the threat to our security posed by weapons of mass destruction has only been reduced, not ended. In recent years, with U.S. leadership, much has been accomplished. Russian warheads no longer target our homes. The last missile silos in Ukraine are being planted over with sunflowers, and nuclear weapons have also been removed from Belarus and Kazakstan. North Korea's nuclear weapons program has been frozen. The Nuclear Nonproliferation Treaty has been extended. A comprehensive ban on nuclear tests has been approved.

And we are continuing the job begun under President Bush of ensuring that Iraq's capacity to produce weapons of mass destruction is thoroughly and verifiably dismantled.

The President's budget empowers us to build on these steps. It provides the resources we need to seek further reductions in nuclear stockpiles, to help assure the safe handling of nuclear materials, to back international inspections of other countries' nuclear programs, and to implement the agreements we have reached.

The President's budget also reflects America's role as the indispensable nation in promoting international security and peace. Our largest single program is in support of the peace process in the Middle East. Even here, the price tag does not compare to the cost to us and to our friends if that strategic region should once again erupt in war. The oil crisis caused by fighting there in 1973 threw our economy into a tailspin, caused inflation to soar and resulted in gas lines that stretched for miles.

Today, as a result of courageous leaders in the region, and persistent American diplomacy, the peace process launched by Secretary Baker has been sustained. Israel has signed landmark agreements with Jordan and the Palestinian authorities. And as the recent pact on Hebron illustrates, the movement towards peace continues despite episodes of violence, outbreaks of terrorism and a tragic assassination.

As Secretary of State, I will ensure that America continues to stand with the peacemakers and against the bombthrowers in this strategic region. That is in America's interests; it is consistent with the commitments we have made; it reflects the kind of people we are; and it is right.

Because the United States has unique capabilities and unmatched power, it is natural that others turn to us in time of emergency. We have an unlimited number of opportunities to act. But we do not have unlimited resources, nor unlimited responsibilities. We are not a charity or a fire department. If we are to protect our own interests and maintain our credibility, we have to weigh our commitments carefully, and be selective and disciplined in what we agree to do.

Recognizing this, we have good reason to strengthen other instruments for responding to emergencies and conflicts, and for addressing the conditions that give rise to those conflicts.

These other instruments include the United Nations, regional organizations and international financial institutions. Together, these entities remove from our shoulders the lion's share of the costs of keeping the peace, maintaining sanctions against rogue states, creating new markets, protecting the environment, caring for refugees and addressing other problems around the globe.

Unfortunately, in recent years, we have fallen behind in our payments to these institutions. We owe about $1 billion to the United Nations and other organizations and almost another $1 billion to the multilateral banks.

In his budget, the President requests enough money to repay many of these obligations. The reason is that these debts hurt America. They erode the capacity of these organizations to carry out programs that serve our interests. They undermine the proposals we have made for reform. And, to those around the world who are hostile to our leadership, they are an open invitation to run America down.

The United States can—and should—lead the way in strengthening and reforming international organizations so that they better serve the world community, and American interests. But if we are to succeed, we must also pay our bills. As in poker, if we want a seat at the table, we have to put chips in the pot.

. . . In closing, let me say that I well understand, as I undertake my new job, that there is no certain formula for ensuring public support for American engagement overseas. Certainly, frankness helps. Consultations with Congress are essential, and we are working with congressional leaders of both parties to an unprecedented degree. But we Americans are brutally fair. As President Kennedy observed after the Bay of Pigs, success has a thousand fathers, while defeat is an orphan. Ultimately, we will be judged not by our rhetoric or our rationales, but by our results.

The reality is that Americans have always been ambivalent about activism abroad. At the end of World War I, an American Army officer, stuck in Europe while the diplomats haggled at Versailles, wrote to his future wife about his yearning to go home: "None of us care if the Russian government is red or not [or] whether the king of Lollipops slaughters his subjects." Thirty years later, that same man—Harry Truman—would lead America in the final stages of another great war.

In the aftermath of that conflict, it was not enough to say that what we were against had failed. Leaders such as Truman, Marshall and Vandenberg were determined to build a lasting peace. And together with our allies, they forged a set of institutions that would defend freedom, rebuild economies, uphold law and preserve peace.

Today, the greatest danger to America is not some foreign enemy; it is the possibility that we will ignore the example of that generation; that we will succumb to the temptation of isolation; neglect the military and diplomatic resources that keep us strong; and forget the fundamental lesson of this century, which is that problems abroad, if left unattended, will all too often come home to America.

A decade or two from now, we will be known as the neo-isolationists who allowed totalitarianism and fascism to rise again or as the generation that solidified the global triumph of democratic principles. We will be known as the neo-protectionists whose lack of vision produced financial chaos or as the generation that laid the groundwork for rising prosperity around the world. We will be known as the world-class ditherers who stood by while the seeds of renewed global conflict were sown or as the generation that took strong measures to deter aggression, control nuclear arms and keep the peace.

There is no certain roadmap to success, either for individuals or for generations. Ultimately, it is a matter of judgment, a question of choice. In making that choice, let us remember that there is not a page of American history of which we are proud that was authored by a chronic complainer or prophet of despair. We are doers.

We have a responsibility in our time, as others have had in theirs, not to be prisoners of history, but to shape history. A responsibility to use and defend our own freedom, and to help others who share our aspirations for liberty, peace and the quiet miracle of a normal life. To that end, I pledge my own best efforts, and solicit yours.

THE FORUM FOR INTERNATIONAL POLICY, ISSUE BRIEF

America's Diplomacy: It Must Be Present in Every Country, Every Day

PRINCIPAL AUTHOR: ERIC D.K. MELBY*

PRESIDENT CLINTON shortly will ask a distinguished American to be his new Secretary of State. This individual would do America—and the world—an enormous service by conditioning his or her response on a solemn commitment by the President to work with Congress to provide the resources necessary to conduct a full-fledged diplomacy. The next Secretary of State must, of course, be able to articulate and carry out a coherent foreign policy. But without substantially increased resources, the next Secretary will preside over an increasingly hollow foreign affairs machinery. Thus, the new Secretary, resolutely supported by the President, must put forward a convincing case for increased resources—and have the stature and stamina to fight for these resources, within the Administration, on Capitol Hill and before the American people.

The U.S. exerts leadership and influence abroad through a varying combination of diplomacy, economic assistance and military force. Neither military force, the ultimate extension of power, nor economic assistance, which should always be applied selectively, can be used on a daily basis. Diplomacy, broadly construed, works around the clock, day in and day out, to protect America's global interests.

For several years, the United States has attempted to project diplomatic power on the cheap, closing diplomatic posts in important countries (e.g., Poland, Indonesia, Mexico, Brazil and the Philippines), cutting diplomatic personnel overseas, reneging on financial oblig-

---

*Eric D.K. Melby is a Senior Associate at the Forum for International Policy. He was on the National Security Council staff from 1987–1993 and has also served with the Department of State and AID.

ations to multilateral institutions we helped create and slashing levels of foreign assistance. While we must continue to seek ways to use resources more effectively, it is time to stop cutting the sinews of our diplomacy. Congress, in an admirable quest to reduce the federal deficit, unfortunately has succumbed to the myth that our diplomacy is bloated and wasteful and thus ripe for budget cuts. America's facilities and representatives overseas are a critical part of shaping the image others have of America. To be treated like the superpower we are, we must project an image of a superpower. This can neither be done on the cheap nor in the current manner—shabby buildings, outmoded technology, restricted budgets. The President must take the lead in convincing Congress to reverse this trend. Both he and his new Secretary of State must be determined and tireless advocates before Congress and the American people.

We expect much from our diplomatic effort. American diplomats overseas gather and analyze information, persuade and advocate, promote American policy and values (political and commercial) and, not least, assist Americans overseas, many of them in trouble (last year there were 233,000 inquiries worldwide about missing Americans and some 30,000 Americans died overseas). American diplomacy is the front line of the battle against terrorism and the proliferation of dangerous weapons and drugs. It is also the front line of the campaign for democracy and human rights and for open markets and reduced trade barriers (creating several hundreds of thousands of well-paying jobs at home in the process). It is through diplomacy that we build solid ties with our friends and allies and, as important, reach out to our adversaries to conduct the nation's foreign policy. Effective diplomacy requires learning foreign languages, understanding foreign cultures and a willingness to live and work in often strenuous and, occasionally, perilous circumstances. (Since 1945, more U.S. ambassadors than generals have been killed in the service of their country.) It can take years of training and experience for a diplomat to become highly effective. Diplomacy is primarily a contact business and contacts need to be nurtured continually to be effective.

For forty-five years after the end of World War II, fear of the Soviet Union was one of the strongest assets we had in convincing other countries to support American views. With the collapse of communism in 1989, that useful focus disappeared. Today, as the only superpower, we elicit contradictory sentiments. We are viewed simultaneously with suspicion and are expected to exert strong, consistent global leadership. Our actions in recent years—cutting resources for international affairs and questioning whether we want to lead the world—puzzle friend and foe, and run counter to the vital national interests we have defended since 1941.

A recent University of Maryland poll shows that the average American believes we spend 18% of the federal budget on foreign affairs, while thinking we should spend only 6%. In reality, foreign affairs spending, the bully pulpit of America's strength overseas, is now only 1% of the federal budget—a little more than one penny of every federal tax dollar. Today we spend a total of $18 billion on foreign aid, on operating our foreign affairs agencies, and on contributions to the United Nations and other international institutions. This is a stunning cut of more than 50%, adjusted for inflation, from the amount we spent in 1984 for the same activities.

With the collapse of communism and the end of the Cold War, it is understandable that the Pentagon's budget has come to reflect the new realities. However, those same realities argue that we increase rather than slash resources for American diplomacy, the success of which will make it less likely that Americans have to go abroad in uniform. The collapse of communism has resulted in some twenty new countries; the American flag needs to fly briskly in these countries. It has also shifted attention to difficult issues such as terrorism, drugs, regional conflicts and the environment. An emaciated foreign affairs budget means there is little ability to respond rationally to these issues, much less the inevitable crises which demand immediate attention.

As international trade grows and market economies flourish, American goods, services and technology increasingly are in demand. American business has a right to expect the help of American diplomats in the most promising regions of the emerging global marketplace. We are not talking about Paris, London or Tokyo; rather, it is places such as Calcutta, Harare and Almaty. These are not comfortable diplomatic assignments which some in Congress love to deride.

These are tough assignments requiring skilled, experienced men and women of character, with a sense of adventure and a commitment to expanding American diplomatic and commercial interests and values.

Regrettably we are reining in our diplomatic presence overseas at the very moment we should expand it. We are doing the same to multilateral institutions such as the United Nations and the Organization for Economic Cooperation and Development, institutions which are cost-effective instruments of American policy when we have the creativity and wisdom to use them correctly. We currently owe the UN and other international organizations more than $2 billion. Our ability to influence these bodies is directly related to our willingness to honor debts we incurred freely.

It is difficult to overstate the critical importance of the next four years for the state of American diplomacy. The President can leave his successor with a finely honed foreign policy instrument capable of understanding and interpreting the new global realities and of projecting American influence. Or he can leave a hollow international affairs corps whose inadequacy will only become evident when it is too late. The former requires forceful and consistent Presidential leadership to convince Congress and the American people why diplomatic readiness is as vital as military readiness—and why neither can be done on the cheap. We have been conducting cut-rate, sporadic diplomacy when the times demand full price, daily diplomacy. The President and his next Secretary of State must be articulate and unrelenting champions for a strong American diplomatic establishment. Our vital national interests demand that American diplomacy be present in every country, every day.

Background Materials

STEPHEN S. ROSENFELD

NICKEL-AND-DIMING FOREIGN POLICY

Washington Post, January 17, 1997

THIS MUCH you can say for the failure of the American government to provide the resources to support our far-flung international interests. The failure reflects a grim success of bipartisanship. Both parties and both political branches fell down.

Republican George Bush, touted as the foreign policy maestro, could not keep a dreaming Democratic Congress from prematurely concluding that the end of the Cold War permitted us to stint on official and public diplomacy and on development.

Democrat Bill Clinton earned his own demerits for indicating to an even more negligent Republican Congress that to balance the budget in the year 2002 international-affairs spending, already down a quarter from the '80s average, would fall by as much more.

Bush at least, in 1990, got Congress to fence off the part of the budget devoted to international affairs from diversion to alternative spending. But a distracted Clinton, a year ago, agreed to put a floor under the national defense budget even as he let international affairs be grouped with non-defense discretionary expenditures. His own budget office then targeted this category for reductions. The State Department's subsequent pleas for protection within a more expansive "national security" category were ignored.

Here I draw on a crisp summons to global duty hatched at this inaugural moment by the Brookings Institution and the Council on Foreign Relations. This right-minded internationalist gang means to rally a constituency for the fund-raising appeals coming concurrently from the sitting and designated secretaries of state. Their report is called "Financing American Leadership," American leadership being the professed banner of most Americans on the right as well as the left. Pulled together by former diplomat Richard Moose, its co-chairs are former liberal Democratic congressman Stephen Solarz, whom you might expect to be aboard, and former conservative Republican congressman Mickey Edwards, whom you might not. The report defines the responsible bipartisan consensus that has been lacking since the Cold War ended.

In fact, the whole way we finance our international policies is unbalanced. The military takes and deserves the lion's share. But surely there is some reasonable point of proportionality—10 percent of defense?—below which civilian non-intelligence international affairs spending should not be allowed to fall. Nor have I ever heard a good reason why the intelligence agencies draw large and apparently expanding and little-overseen sums—now toward $30 billion—even as the well-probed foreign policy agencies are nickel-and-dimed. In fiscal 1997 they received $18 billion, and for 1998 the Clinton administration is seeking only a cautious billion more. It ought to be asking unapologetically for at least an extra two.

You do not have to wave a flag for the State Department to grasp the common-sense proposition that the already-advanced thinning of the State infrastructure shrinks the capacity to promote vital American interests and contributes to an image of decline and withdrawal.

No less crippling, the new report suggests, are the constraints on practical presidential options. To stabilize Haiti, economic support was reduced to Turkey, a critical regional country. Aid to the West Bank had to be drained from the Central American peace account. Refugee care in Rwanda took funds from democracy-building elsewhere in Africa. For lack of ready money to monitor a Kurdish cease-fire in northern Iraq, Saddam Hussein was handed a pretext to send in his own forces—"a move which culminated in U.S. military action costing multiples of the originally needed sum."

Sen. Richard Lugar assails what he sees as a expedient bipartisan "fiction" that international spending can be cut with impunity: "As important as balancing the budget is, it will not happen if American disengagement from the world results in nuclear terrorism, an international trade war, an international energy crisis, a major regional conflict requiring U.S. intervention or some other preventable disaster that undermines our security and prosperity."

Treading on ground where secretaries of state hesitate to go, this outsiders' report puts the onus directly on President Clinton. He is urged first to ask for adequate funding, then to go to the people and then to address Congress. To grease the process, a deal on restructuring the foreign affairs agencies—a congressional passion—is recommended, and a billion dollars' worth of legitimate reform is tossed in.

As a second Clinton term begins, no great foreign policy debate is going on, and none is needed. There is no single great "vision" available, but there is broad agreement that our interests require well-considered engagement to tend to a host of issues that won't stand still. For that we need not so much a master plan as an attitude of alertness and an apparatus that lets us try to stay ahead of the curve. This is what a good foreign policy can do. This is why we cannot afford to go on the cheap.

MICKEY EDWARDS AND STEPHEN J. SOLARZ

RESOURCES FOR INTERNATIONAL AFFAIRS

THE COLD WAR was won not just by Western military might but by America's efforts to forge a strong community of democratic, prosperous, and stable countries. U.S. diplomacy and foreign assistance played crucial roles. Now, in our efforts to balance the budget, we unnecessarily risk demolishing those very tools of global influence.

To take a specific example from the recent headlines, one place where the negative consequences could soon be felt is Zaire. The United States is showing little interest in crafting strategies to end that African country's civil war—partly because there are no funds available to pay our share of any U.N. peacekeeping or election-monitoring costs that would be incurred under a peace plan there.

Apart from defense, international affairs is the only major category of federal spending to have declined in real terms over the 1990s. It is costing the United States $19 billion in 1997, nearly 20 percent less in real terms than the 1980s average. That is barely a penny on the federal dollar. It would decline another 15 percent by 2002 under the president's new budget proposal, and by even more under Congress's deficit-elimination plan of last year.

That $19 billion supports a remarkable variety of important activities. They include: U.S. diplomacy and export promotion programs worldwide; peacemaking efforts in the Balkans and the Middle East; child survival programs and humanitarian relief in Africa and Asia; the prevention of nuclear proliferation in North Korea and the Persian Gulf; support for democracy and market reforms in the former Soviet Union; and various efforts of the United Nations and World Bank.

With the end of the Cold War, some savings in foreign assistance have been possible. Allies like the Philippines, Greece, and Turkey that previously received substantial amounts of security aid either no longer face the threats or no longer provide the absolutely critical U.S. military access they once did. Also, some developing countries, particularly in East Asia and South America, have advanced enough economically that they no longer need our help. Reforms in how we provide foreign assistance and conduct diplomacy could save additional sums. But the cuts in spending have now gone too far, jeopardizing our strategic and economic interests. We are starting to close State Department facilities overseas, including some embassies, and are unable to open enough new consulates to help American business, even in countries with huge markets like China.

We have been forced to be too selective about which violence-torn African and Central American countries to help stabilize and rebuild. For lack of funds, we have passed up opportunities to provide assistance to nongovernmental organizations in Cuba and China bent on furthering human rights and democracy.

To examine such distressing trends, the Brookings Institution and the Council on Foreign Relations recently convened a bipartisan task force on resources for U.S. foreign affairs. The task force, whose recommendations were endorsed by several former secretaries of state and defense, has concluded that the 1997 international spending level of $19 billion should rise to at least $21 billion in 1998 and be adjusted for inflation thereafter.

Little will happen, however, without presidential leadership. So far, the signals are mixed. President Clinton forcefully articulated the need for adequate resources in his State of the Union Address. He then asked Congress for a modest increase in budget authority for 1998 that will suffice to keep actual spending near the real 1997 level. Unfortunately, his budget plans for subsequent years would put spending back on a downward path. Fortunately, there is still time to adjust them.

But money alone is not enough; the president must also indicate a willingness to work with Congress to restructure this country's foreign policy machinery for the post–Cold War world. Reforms should be undertaken in the State Department, Agency for International Development, U.S. Information Agency, and Arms Control and Disarmament Agency—in their own right and to gain Congress's support for adequate resources. We can afford as a nation to do more than we are at present; we cannot afford to do less.

Former Congressmen Mickey Edwards (R-OK) and Stephen Solarz (D-NY) released their Task Force's report in January.

Notes